MW00582253

יהוה

# MASONIC TRAVELER

*Essays and Commentary*
*2005-2009*
*Gregory Stewart 32° R :. A :. M :.*
MMBBFMN

*Once, when thought came to me of the things that are and my thinking soared high and my bodily senses were restrained, like someone heavy from sleep from to much eating or toil of the body, an enormous being completely unbound in size seemed to appear to me and call my name and say to me:*

*"What do you want to hear and see?  What do you want to learn and know from your understanding?"*

*Hermetica*

*Study what thou art,*
*whereof thou art a part,*
*what thou knowest of this art,*
*this is really what thou art.*
*All that is without thee is also within,*
*thus wrote Trismosin*

*Alchemical Wanderings*

Published by a brother in Freemasonry
for the future of Freemasonry.

First Printing 2010

Masonic Traveler - Essays and Commentary
ISBN# 978-0-615-35918-2

Copyright ©2010 by Gregory Stewart

All content is representative of the author and
does not represent the opinions of any regular or
irregular Masonic body and/or Grand Lodge.

Published by FreemasonInformation.com
Encino, California
United States of America
www.freemasoninformation.com

Any reproduction of this book, in part or in full,
without the expressed written permission of
Gregory Stewart is strictly prohibited.

©2010 Gregory Stewart – All Rights Reserved

Continue the conversation online at
twitter.com/masonictraveler
and on
facebook.com/masonictraveler

Artwork courtsey of Shag ©2000, 2010 Josh Agle

This book is dedicate to my loving wife Diane and my wonderful sons Kristian and Nathaniel.

The work of the book is dedicated to all brothers, past, present, and future, that carried the torch seeking knowledge and wisdom, forever searching for the lost master's word, no matter their discipline.

My special thanks to Tim Bryce for his years of mentorship and unwavering dedication to the craft. To Daniel Mayhew, who helped shape and hone my spiritual mind through many discussions and reality checks over the years. To Terence Satchell for his Masonic eye and editorial review, and to Fred Miliken for his unwavering support, to Professor Margaret Jacob, of UCLA, for the inspiration to re-imagine Freemasonry in the 21st Century, and lastly to my good friend and dear brother Dean Kennedy for his persistence.

# TABLE OF CONTENTS

# INTRODUCTION

*by*
*Tim Bryce*

When we are raised to the sublime degree of Master Mason we are admonished to seek "further light." This means to ponder, to question, to seek answers and to grow and evolve as a species. Undoubtedly, this expression originated from the "Age of Enlightenment" in the 18th century which was fueled by Masonic thought and resulted in dramatic advancements in government, education, the arts and sciences, and basic God-given unalienable rights, such as freedom. This cultural period did not discourage creative thought, but rather unleashed it in the form of a proliferation of authors, artists, explorers, inventors, scientists, pioneers, and leaders. All of this because man's ability to reason was placed on a pedestal and cherished. Basically, it encouraged people to lead a meaningful life, not slave-like. It is no small wonder Freemasonry flourished during this period and spread around the world like the locust.

After conquering continents, ignorance, many diseases, and himself (on more than one occasion), man slowed down to enjoy the fruits of his labor, and thus began the Dark Ages of the fraternity as it evolved into more of a social club as opposed to an institution for enlightenment. Petty politics crept into Freemasonry resulting in bureaucracies and fiefdoms replacing temples of learning and brotherhood, and apathy superseding initiative. And membership in the fraternity plummeted.

Fortunately, we are at the dawn of a Masonic Renaissance. The word "Renaissance" is French for "rebirth" and refers to the intellectual and economic changes that occurred in Europe from the fourteenth through the sixteenth centuries. During this period, Europe emerged from the economic stagnation of the Middle Ages and experienced a time of financial and intellectual growth. This is precisely what is beginning to happen to Freemasonry: a return to enlightenment.

Thanks to new technologies, man now has the means to communicate faster and more  precisely than ever before. It is now within our power to find answers to our questions  within seconds, minutes or hours, as opposed to waiting days, weeks, months, or years. This has stimulated thought and debate and is the impetus for our Renaissance. Such thought and dialog though does not sit well with those who see it as a threat to their  authority and censorship is occasionally invoked, which would probably have been unimaginative to our Masonic forefathers. You cannot be enlightened if you are not allowed to challenge the status quo and express new ideas.

Fortunately, there is a new generation of Masons emerging who bear a close resemblance to our 18th century predecessors. We are now seeing men join the fraternity who are not so much interested in joining a club, but rather for enlightenment. Not surprising, Traditional Observance Lodges ("TO") are springing  up as an attempt to recapture the original mystique of Masonry. In such Lodges,  there is less emphasis on rushing through the three degrees, and more on studying and  growing morally and intellectually, which is a throwback to another era.

New Masonic authors are also surfacing who not only examine our past, but consider our destiny. Like their forefathers, they dare to ask, "Why?" This is leading them to research and study the history and underpinnings of the fraternity in the hopes of promoting its success into the future.

Why this sudden burst of intellectual curiosity? I'm not sure. I can only assume people are looking for more meaning to their lives and Freemasonry represents a fountainhead of long-lost information which is only now being rediscovered. Their search is not about the meaning of life, as much as it is about morality and making the world a better place, a much more global perspective.

Renaissance Masons are also cognizant of the legacy they will leave behind as a result of their stewardship. They are keenly aware their successors will be judging them as either the generation who dropped the ball, or picked it up and ran with it for a touchdown.

Bro. Greg Stewart is a Renaissance Mason with a ravenous curiosity for all things Masonic. I have had the honor and privilege of knowing him for the last few years and know him to be a man of integrity and sincerity. His writings in this book are thought-provoking and reflect the conscious of a True Mason, one who is endeavoring to fulfill his quest for "further light."

Tim Bryce, PM, MPS, MMBBFMN
Palm Harbor, Florida, USA
October 2009

# FOREWORD

February 2010

In the years of my journey as a Freemason, I have learned much. I have had the opportunity to communicate with Masons around the world, to have conversations with Prince Hall Brothers, share thoughts and correspondence with Co-Masonic Brothers, and develop associations with a number of, non-Masonic but loosely affiliated, Rites, Societies, and Orders. This, in essence, broadened my once narrow Masonic world view to a wider field of possibility that Masonry is capable of being. It has been an amazing experience and one that I believe has only just begun.

This book is a culmination of those interactions and experiences and the story of the Masonic Traveler.

I'm glad you have joined me in my journey. This book originated out of a group of posts made on the Masonic Traveler blog between 2005 and 2008. The blog began as a way for me to be active in Freemasonry in a time that had otherwise kept me away from the lodge. It was not for a lack of interest but a culmination of life and career that demanded precedent. In that period I did find some time to further my search for Masonic Light. It became an adventure of sorts, a journey from west to east and back again, through books, interactions with brothers, and on the web. I felt that to be a Mason, I needed to immerse myself in knowing what that meant. And while on that journey I needed to talk about it and share my discoveries and musing. In that period the Masonic Traveler was born.

Having reached a cross road now as the Masonic Traveler blog merges with its progenitor web site freemasoninformation.com, which I created at about the same time, I felt that a compilation of some of the more memorable essays made in those years should see a more permanent home in print. In some cases they have been revised, in others entirely re-written. Also, there are a few unpublished works that cross paths with other endeavors that I have undertaken in that time. It challenges what we consider normal and dares to think beyond the convention of a square ruled box and compass inscribed circle. The work is entirely my opinion or my reaction to the opinion of others and in some cases a healthy dose of both. The essays are my observations to some of the interesting questions I found myself asking. They are, in a sense the culmination of my Masonic Travels.

Working through this material, some specific themes have surfaced and ingrained in me a particular set of ideas about the fraternity that I believe are overlooked by a wide majority of the modern Masonic body. This has labeled me as a heretic by some and as being misinformed by others to which sadly I cannot argue against. What I can attest to is the breadth of fraternity that, in its own way, appreciates this analysis and exploration. To you, I offer my findings and thoughts to help you on your own quest and to generate thought and discussion.

Of all the conclusions I have come to the most prominent

to me is that the system of Freemasonry today is not merely one of a weekly social hour or "fish fry" as is so often the accusation, but instead a rich philosophical society with fingers both in the "third way" of faith and in the "new age" idea of a metaphysical spiritual development. How else could you describe an initiation order that brings a man from darkness to light, and raises a candidate from an allegorical death? And, to make the tradition all the more relevant is the fact that it has existed in this way for nearly 300 recorded years with a veiled pre-history that goes back for, I believe, at least another 300. Following these bread crumbs through the forest has lead me to some interesting conclusions perhaps to be explored in more depth in the future. Needless to say, the experience has been about my journey and not the destination I've reached.

In the less conjectural side of this work several things have happened as a result of this odyssey. As life has normalized my activity in lodge has increased and my understanding of the fraternity in both the past aspect and the present aspect has grown far beyond I even imagined it could. The why and how of it has been answered, for me, and its given me ample time to think about the future of the Royal Art. From this understanding a great affection for it has blossomed, as well as a heightened sense of what it means to be a member of it. And, in that ever growing sense, I have realized that it is in each of our hands to understand what it means and to promulgate and contribute to its growth and future. That each of us has a part to contribute to the whole.

With that in mind, I hope that this body of my Masonic musing inspires you to a greater understanding of why we are Masons and to a renewed interest in being a Freemason, that it will inspire your Masonic journey, whether far down the road or at its starting point.

And to the non Mason reading this book at the threshold of encountering the fraternity, I hope this text helps further your understanding of it in the 21st Century.

To my brothers of the square and compass, this work I humbly offer to you to further your travels.

**Vivat :. Vivat :. Vivat :.**

Greg Stewart
*Masonic Traveler*

# I
# WHAT IS A
# FREEMASON?

*Freemasons nurture and grow the divine spark in
humanity through the tenants of Brotherly Love,
Relief, and Truth.*

A Freemason is a man who in searching for life's ineffable
questions, finds his way into the company of fellow seekers.
Comprised of men from every nation, races, social and economic
level, all hold similar ideals and beliefs. The uniting idea is a faith
in the divine founded in the certitude in an afterlife. This "belief" is
grounded by certain landmark tenants and virtues which ultimately
lead in exploration of those invisible questions, leading ultimately to
the betterment of all mankind.

Traditionally a male organization, Freemasons exist in most
every country around the world guided by three principals: Brotherly
Love, Relief, and Truth. The Fraternity is open to all men, with a
belief in the divine, a passion towards humanity, and a desire to
better themselves. Foremost is the practice of Brotherly Love, not just
towards fellow Freemason's, but towards all mankind for the purpose
of unity and cooperation. Within the lodge, the bonds made through
fellowship are vitally important steps towards a better understanding
one another. Outside of the lodge, Brotherly Love leads to a greater
degree of understanding and compassion towards all men. Coming

to the aid of those in true need, Relief is a second light that serves as a sanctuary for the weary and distressed, what ever the cause to those in need, whether it be poverty, infirmity or what ever their ailment. And Truth, whose search is unending, becomes its own virtue by relating to the nature of man and his transcendental state. Truth does not conform to any specific dogmatic practice of law instead accepting all faiths as sacred. Freemasons nurture and grow the divine spark in humanity through the tenants of Brotherly love, Relief and Truth.

But, why exist for the betterment of mankind? For too long man has looked through varying degrees of authority for the answers to those unanswerable questions, "what is our nature and purpose" asked since time immemorial. By looking to answer those questions, Freemasons have found, instead the virtue in which the answers reside. To help frame the questions, Freemasons rely on four of the cardinal virtues, which are Temperance, Fortitude, Prudence, and Justice. Temperance to suppresses our personal extremes, and promote modesty, Fortitude to keep good faith and careful watch ourselves, Prudence which keeps the perils of corruption in mind, and Justice which gives each their sense of due not stealing from another. By applying these virtues, the questions become transparent and unanswerable in terms of everyday ideas, instead they take on internal meaning, answerable only in the personal application of the virtues. The idea of personal growth this way is paramount to the craft, taught through lessons in allegory and symbols. The significance of learning this way is to convey their meaning symbolically, fostering individual introspection of their meaning. Exploration of these virtues is only part of the foundation of a Freemason with more enumerated throughout the allegorical degrees, all working to shape those who seek its light.

But the quest for answers is not lead by virtue alone. What many outside consider a barrier, is instead one of the strongest aspects of

Freemasonry. Open to all faiths, Freemasonry has certain "landmarks" by which they live. One landmark in-particular is an acknowledged faith in God. Seeing the true nature of man through his works, a Freemason finds divine nature to be majestic in its meaning. But, to discuss faith, it would be problematic to not acknowledge the role of religion in the craft. Without any rule or requirement, Freemasonry neither prescribes to nor inflicts doctrinal controls over a member's beliefs, ideas, or duties, but instead builds on the nature of good men; it only requires a simple profession of faith. Within Freemasonry there are no cannons of absolute law or moral leader as with a church congregation. Instead within each body of Freemasonry, democracy rules along with the sacred books of law, as prescribed to by each member's faith. These books represent the backgrounds of the membership and the foundations from which they come, serving to link Freemasons to the transcendent. However, within the lodge, the conflicts of the sacred volumes are shunned, instead to embrace their celebration of the divine. What this represents is an open democratic society governed by mutual respect, advocating unity and harmony. No where is their represented malice or disunion, instead, men of all faiths are encouraged to make a harmonious fellowship.

As such, the inclusion of all faiths has made tremendous enemies. The diligent observer can easily find dissent from all faiths about the brotherhood of Freemasonry. Some examples are as recent as tracts written by the Pope of the Catholic Church, denouncing membership as being in disharmony with Christian faith. Also, standing against the gentle craft are imams of Islam, pastors of protestant Christianity, and rabbi's of Judaism. The unique thing to all these groups is their agreement that their members should not join the fraternity and shun it as heretical. Their reasoning is that Freemasonry acts as a surrogate to religion, replacing their doctrines of faith. But reason shows us otherwise, as masonry builds on the tenants of all faith, embracing the primitive aspects of each faith, in that all faiths are sacrosanct.

Freemasons work to smooth the rough stone edge indifference to create a vibrant and living craft. Neither libertines, racists, nor atheists by creed, Freemasons should not suffer it to exist within its body. Therefore, it is accurate to say that masons are not irreligious; to the contrary their mandate is a belief in the divine. The obligations taken as Freemasons do nothing to stand in the way of our family, our religion, or our civic participation, rather it necessitates our participation in all of these and more by advocating charity through brotherly love. Of this, love of our neighbor is to be paramount in our mind. We are, in fact, encouraged to perform our duties to God, our neighbor, and ourselves daily. Our fraternal bonds are made sacred by oaths and obligations between men, making us stronger and united in purpose. Those oaths make the bonds stronger and the bonds make the men stronger.

Freemasonry strives in its membership to bring like minded men together to explore the four cardinal virtues in hopes to glimpse the divine transcendence of God. Existing in all lands membership relies on the members own free will and accord, each in his search for illumination through the hands of the divine. A Freemason believes in the brotherhood of man and fatherhood of a compassionate deity. Surrounded by like minded men, masons are dedicated to Brotherly Love, Relief, and Truth, believing in their universality of the sacred and divine for the betterment of mankind.

# II
# DIGGING

*...ideas turned to a deeper question of transcending the spheres of man and his consciousness to reach and cross over the threshold of the spirit...*

Of late I have been digging. Digging into the history of Freemasonry to uncover more of where we came from and why we exist. Why I have been digging is of a greater interest as my purpose was to better understand what we are doing, and why we do it. Freemasonry, as practiced today, is an ancient institution with a lineage that we can trace to a minimum of 300 years in our past. But in those years it has grown and evolved in a self manufactured crucible of tangible absolutes. But how is this possible? How can an institution appear out of nowhere and then go on to touch so many of our lives today? This growth, and its influence on several key areas of our modern life, happened with little cohesive understanding of why. It is out of this curiosity that prompted my quest. And, by digging through these questions, I have come to some perhaps unconventional conclusions.

One area that I have found the greatest resonance with is how an organization so steeped in symbolism and allegory could have so few tangible earmarks to its previous life, that at its very foundation evidence seems to exist of institutions of similar character but with very few marks to connect its points. Several authors and scholars have made great strides to connect the dots, some with speculative suggestions, and others with some tangible clues. Through them all, however, there seems to be a consensus that something came before. What I have come to see is that at some point, early in the 1600's, Freemason and Rosicrucian thought crossed paths and likely merged for a time together to form a large degree of esoteric (occult) and organizational knowledge. This does not mean to denigrate the ancient assumption of the stone mason guilds and the obvious connections between modern Freemasonry and these ancient builders; To the contrary, it seems that at some point these guilds became infused with something more than mere allegories. Now, before you run off and call me a witch or a heretic, there was a period of time that the occult did not have the overt assumption of some sort of consorting with the devil (though the dominate faiths of today would have you believe otherwise). The church, however, would have you believe otherwise, then and now, and the only connection to the divine was through their agency. It was in this climate that eventually Protestantism and Christian mysticism would emerge and become a "third" way to knowing God. The occult was then perceived to be a secret knowledge, a mixing of angels, demons, and spiritual worlds between the physical earth and the celestial divine realm where God dwelt. Few dared to explore this realm of ideas that had for centuries been the secret science of magus, or magicians, and the magick that they explored was unknown to most and something we today take for granted.

Others have concluded and suggested that this "magick" had much to do with the understanding of mathematics (specifically the study and understanding of geometry and chemistry). The art of astrology, the craft of making and transmuting metals in alchemy, the mystery of math and geometry were not new in the Renaissance, but they were limited to those who had access to discoveries of these ancient ideas which became tied into the work that the Free

Stone masons were endeavoring in. Further, that the builders of the house of GOD, using this sacred geometry, came to see their work as transcendent to the confines of earth reaching into the heavens. This is truly a romantic vision that speaks little to the toilsome work of chisel to stone in works that could take centuries to complete, yet still the guilds of builders have played prominently into this fraternity where few today could so artfully shape these masterpieces.

From these Free Stone Masons, who had not yet fully manifested the ritualized degrees of our understanding today, we have built a system that has adopted their "lodges" and meetings (festive boards) and evolved them to become our temples of this art whereby we could share their memory that had become universal amongst them. We know that as time progressed their craft became more diluted with an expanding labor force of "accepted" numbers who diminished the physical art of building by admitting more and more "speculative" builders, which gradually evolved the idea of temples into the moral allegories of building internally what had once been an external transformation. These ideas came from the alchemists and proto scientists who brought an air of this Hermetic Magick born anew in the coalesced ideas of the Rosicrucian movement, to manifest in the writing of texts such a the Fama Fraternitas. It is from this Rosicrucian text that put into words the ideas that had been germinating already for hundreds of years before hand with the experimentation of countless alchemists in both physical chemistry and transformational mysticism. From the likes of Fludd, Dee, Agrippa, Paracelsus, Bacon, Bruno, Richelun, Ficino, and others who discoveries contemplated and challenged the hierarchies of monarchy and Christianity that developed over time a different perspective of the divine, some of whom burned at the stake for it. The very idea of exploring these notions were considered as heresy as they were contrary to the teachings of the ever-present Roman Catholic Church, the burgeoning Protestant reformation, and the Anglican Church, and necessitated an air of secrecy and fraternity to explore them. Over time these alchemists moved past the exploration of turning lead into gold, and their ideas turned to a deeper question of transcending the spheres of man and his consciousness to reach and cross over the threshold of the spirit to transcend what the church's notion of God was and experience it personally to connect with the Great Architect of the Universe through their own processes and practices. To do this though required an understanding of and a methodology to harness both angels and demons to move from the spheres of the earth and the heavens into the realm of the Divine.

More importantly, with this exploration is the notion of the discovery itself. In this exploration came the question: "does the final answer mean as much as the process of seeking it in the first place?" And with the fictions and facts so intermingled and enmeshed in one another, as they separate out, do they then contribute themselves some piece to the puzzle that ultimately is the mystery?

It is because of these questions that I keep digging, and through the tailings of the past start to form the picture of the present within which Freemasonry will coalesce into our own reality; that is the Masonic Fraternity.

# III
# THE
# BEEHIVE

*If all of the bees forget their labors and fail to tend to their obligations, the system falls apart and the hive perishes...*

In the book *"The Newly Made Mason"* Freemasonry is defined as the culmination of all things Masonic[1]. The term Freemasonry has become the crystallized identification of the external perception of what we have made the collected fraternity to represent. That Freemasonry is religion, science, allegory, symbol, fraternity, and brotherhood, and that all of these, in their sum and parts, equate to what Freemasonry is. But I often I see Freemasonry referred to as if it were a material object, some tangible substance that we can evaluate empirically as an isolated substance. That thought drove me to ask the question, *"What is Freemasonry?"* There are many definitions that described it, but I soon realized that its meaning did not stem from the sum of its parts in terms of the traditions we hold or the rituals we perform. "Freemasonry" is not the meetings we attend; it is not the aprons we wear, the sparkling jewels or the missions of charity we perform. Freemasonry is the act, or action, by which we labor and not simply a title we give ourselves. This observation becomes clear when looking at the fraternity like a hive or network of activity, governed and run internally as network of bees, each attributing their own small part to build the greater whole.

The philosophical meaning of masonry, as I see it, represents the odyssey of the man on his individual ascent through the degrees towards the inner chamber of his soul. But that answer, ultimately, does nothing to answer the question of whether Freemasonry is anything more than the material nature of its members that assemble to create it and the rules and regulations that we as Freemasons believe are our foundations.

But is Freemasonry not, exclusively, that kind of tangible substance? That it has a physical body with an associated force of will. Perhaps even the term "Freemasonry" is a misnomer, implying it is something corporeal, a person, or granite like institution assuming that all Freemason is working together in one conglomerate body, that "Freemasonry", as an idea, has become a misleading term that fosters a misperception that it is an institution made up of members officers and governing bodies. To say "Freemasonry" implies an infrastructure and/or a corporate entity, which is not inaccurate when looking at the sum of the parts, but that it is more than that and has always been more than that. That those tangibles, though real, are only present to facilitate one thing: a membership existing in harmony together within our societal infrastructure. In fact that Freemasonry is the summation of all of this, and merely a name for the act that we perform and as builders of a spiritual building of the divine house that systemically we refer to as Solomon's Temple, whose greater metaphor is more occulted and obscure.

This idea came to me when considering the symbol of the beehive found in the third degree lecture. In it, the beehive is considered a simple emblem of industry where individuals endeavor industriously in the goings of their lives and there secular participation in society[2]. Simply put that we are to be "busy as a bee" contributing to the whole of our world. The lecture goes on to say that the symbol illustrates our social inter-dependence as one of the strongest bonds of our society saying "mankind was [sic] made dependent on each other for protection and security". Again, that we, in society, are to be busy in our endeavors. It goes on to say "…Thus was man formed for social and active life, the noblest part of the work of God; and he that will so demean himself as not to be endeavoring to add to the common stock of knowledge and understanding, may be deemed a drone In the hive of nature, a useless member of society, and unworthy of our protection as Masons."

Reflecting on this and our role as Masons, I was compelled to see the role of the bee in relation to the hive. In our daily life, we benefit from the bee's behavior, its pollination of plants and production of its wax and sweet honey. In its way it contributes greatly to our environment. But my thoughts turned to the function of the bee internally to the hive. What occurred to me was that the bees were not endeavoring to build trees mountains, or flowers, nor were they endeavoring to stimulate the growth of the flowers that their movement of pollen helps to propagate. The efforts of the bee relate directly to the development of the hive.

Within the hive each bee serves its role and function for the collective growth. Some are born to work, some to fight, some to collect food and provide nourishment. Through and through their efforts contribute individually to tend, build, and grow the collective unit. Simply, the bee does not exist to serve itself, nor construct the world around it. These are, in fact, the benefits of its life and actions shaped by its industry and dedication to the hive. The hive, in this equation, becomes the center of its labor, an ark perhaps, like the ark of Noah; the hive becomes a refuge of peace, prosperity, and tranquility in an otherwise dangerous world. The hive then has a tangible quality then to it, capable of existing without the presence of its inhabitants for a time before its empty combs crumble to dust. Their relationship, the bee to the hive becomes a unique symbiosis sustaining life and home. Without the actions of the bee, who reside within, the hive would not flourish and die.

To the hive then, our Masonic institution has a strong correlation to this idea. That elusive meaning of the word "Freemasonry" then essentially represents the hive and its myriad functions and internal workings, and the Freemasons within it, the bees.

The lesson I have taken away from the symbol of the hive is that we each need to work for that invisible structure supporting and nourishing its growth. Where that work becomes the frenetic activity of the hive and the invisible structure of what we have termed "Freemasonry". If all of the bees forget their labors and fail to tend to their obligations, the system of their home falls apart and the hive perishes. My conclusion here is that the metaphor within the third degree was incomplete, that the industry of the bee was not just to all of society, but to the society to which we reside.

"Freemasonry" is that hive in which all of us labor. Without our individual actions and contributions, and the past actions of our predecessors, we would not have the hive we cherish so dearly today. Collectively, we make up that invisible body of Freemasonry, the leadership, warriors, and harvesters that labor for the betterment of our institution all around. Without our labor, all that would exist is an empty ark of catacombs with vague forgotten symbols lost to the memory of man.

Perhaps in the abstract, Freemasonry is linked to a verb and not a noun, as it truly is the sum of the parts in action and not a title by which to point to. Freemasonry, not as a material object, with a tangible texture or measurable mass but defined as the frenetic energy within. And like that essence of life that is made possible by the unyielding vibration of activity. That growth and progress happens without thought, that it becomes the result of our existence. Like the hive, the peril is when that when vibration of activity stops, so to will the life of the hive stop. Each of us must be vigilant and industrious, inwardly and outwardly, like the bee, as we are forever building our hive of our lodge, contributing to the growth of the world we live in.

# IV
## ANNO
## LUCIS

As a young Mason, I would often come across the reference A.L. when encountering dates of some significance to the fraternity. Lodge founding's, corner stone laying, or charter signatures each with dressed flourish of A.L. followed by an obscure number that did not seem to have any correlation to the thing it referenced. From this curiosity, I began to investigate and explore what the abbreviation meant and its context to the Masonic lexicon.

After a brief investigation what I found was that A.L. is an abbreviation for "Anno Lucis", which is a Latin phrase that translates as "Year of Light". Of a greater interest was the meaning of the term in context to a dating system adopted by early Masonic founders. The oddity of the vas numbers scribed to these monuments was a fixed point in time to the year 4004 B.C.E. The arbitrary number of that date, however, was the product of a certain Bishop Ussher in 1650-54 as the date of the "creation of the world". This little known footnote in Masonic lore and Christian history has an interesting contribution to the myths and mysteries of the fraternity. Bishop Ussher was the Anglican Archbishop of Armagh, in Northern

Ireland, and Primate (first Bishop) of All Ireland between 1625-1656. How Ussher derived the date and its significance is where we find the most interesting, aspect of the date that we use to denote out origins. The 4004 B.C.E. date that Bishop arrived at was based on his analysis of historical (secular) documents and records, along with a close analysis of the bible and other religious texts that he found relevance in. His work produced the text *"Annales Veteris Testamenti, a Prima Mundi Origine Deducti"* ("Annals of the Old Testament, deduced from the first origins of the world"), which was published in 1650 and followed with, Annalium pars postierior in 1654. In this work, he famously claimed, that God created the Earth at nightfall preceding 23 October, 4004 B.C.E.

I still did not understand how this number found its way into Freemasonry which was a bit of a mystery. Ussher's date, then accepted by the church, worked its way into the notes of Genesis, through an inclusion in the margins of the newly printed King James edition of the Holy Bible, which helped spread it into the common knowledge of the age.[1]

Through his work, 4004 B.C.E. (universally applied as 4000 B.C.E.) was then considered to be the beginning of "the world". This date has this become the basis for the Masonic Anno Lucis. How this date is then applied is by adding 4000 to the present year, you derive the calculus of the years since the origin of light 4000 + 2006 becoming 6009 A.L. or six thousand and six years since the year of light. The idea is antiquated and easily questioned by modern scholarship, but in the age it was written, it became accepted as accurate. Interestingly his antiquated resources, many of Ussher's dates correspond to what modern scholarship today has determined to be accurate in history.

The first recorded use of "Anno Lucis" in Freemasonry doesn't appear until 1777 on a certificate issued by the Grand Lodge of England to the Lodge of Alfred which later closed in 1790[2] but not before it had made six early Grand Lodge Officers. Prior to that certificate however, 'Anno Lucis' appeared with varying translations such as Anno Lithotomorum, LAPOR, (year of labor), Anno Lapidariorum (year of movement) and Anno Laotomiae (year of release), all of which appeared in some form on different documents relating to the craft with the same system of dating. Also used on documents in that era time were: A.M. for Anno Masonry (Year of Masonry). But from 1777, "Anno Lucis" becomes the normative usage in more and more documents until it was adopted and put into common use as masonry coalesced into an organized body with orthodox rites and rituals. It became a part of the mythology and nomenclature in Freemasonry.

Today we find Anno Lucis, or A.L., as a common date delineator used on many documents and on corner stones placed around the world to celebrate important foundations. The uses of this 4004/4000 starting point, however, still raises some interesting questions and worth contemplating more deeply as the fraternity and its traditions are linked to older ideas and mystery traditions. Ussher used that time to trace back to what he saw as the beginning of the Christian physical world, but what if in fact he had traced the dating back to the beginning of Western Society? If the origin of the date to Freemasonry is unclear, the date is very specific to the presumed start of creation. Perhaps, like so much else in Freemasonry, this is a symbolic metaphor that we can observe and say that it speaks more of a metaphysical creation, rather than of a physical one. Especially as it is in our origin that we link the date to, or at least the nomenclature that we link institutional foundations with.

Historically we can look back in time and see that in the era of 4004 B.C.E., was in many ways the beginning of our modern civilization in the appearance of the Mesopotamians and Sumerian cultures. Some of their ancient accomplishments, over the centuries of their society, include a developed written language, that we can study and see today, and an organized belief in divine gods beyond their physical space with a pronounced definition of sin that incurred punishment for bad behavior and rewards for good behavior. They also had developed a modern concept of ownership of land, with divisions of wealth and power. Their also existed education, war and recorded dissent within its populace. This is the earliest form of civilization that we can look back to as a vestige of the civilization we have today. This is not to say that Freemasonry is a direct inheritor of this society, but rather that it can perhaps play a role in its mythological ancestry. And from such developed culture and civilization we can find some relationship as builders of the divine temple we can trace on the foundations of this early civilization. As Usser saw this period to be the beginning of the world, we can still link back to this "Year of Light" as we are carefully instructed to forever seek more light.

With that in mind we can find a point to go back to in the shadow of time as we look forward into the future and reverse the metaphor to say that in each founding we establish a new "Year of Light" and recreate Anno Lucis anew. However the Masonic lexicon remembers Anno Lucis, our documents and memorials will forever be adorned with this ancient memory of the beginning, the year of light.

As we explore our history, perhaps we can look back in time and see the dawning of the year of light as we stand in the radiance of its glow today.

# V

# ESOTERICA AND FREEMASONRY

Esoteric - es-uh-ter-ik - adjective.

*Intended for or understood by only a particular group: an esoteric cult. - Synonyms with mysterious. Of or relating to that which is known by a restricted number of people. Confined to a small group: esoteric interests, not publicly disclosed; confidential.*

Masonic Esoterica is an often-debated vein of Freemasonry. Many "traditionalists" argue that the esoteric aspects are merely later additions to a secular fraternity bourn from a mythic past and created as an attempt to lend greater credence to its antiquity and authority.

Some writers, such as Anderson, Mackey, and later Hall, have made great strides in linking allegorical meanings and symbolic teachings to a broader history with an ethereal connection to the past.

Often, this "ethereal" connection is referred to as the ancient mystery schools of antiquity or of a great brotherhood of those who sought a deeper understanding of life than what a mundane existence offered. From these mystery schools of the past come later institutions and movements that have encapsulated their teachings and carried forward their ideals, in most instances separate from other movements of similar tenants. Many of these movements are evident in the Gnostic and Hermetic ideas folded into Freemasonry. The presence of the divine being within us is a part of the silent mantras of degrees practiced from rites and ceremonies developed in an age long ago. Not an external unattainable deity, but an attainable internal one. The Masonic ritual teaches us that the divine exists atop the ladder of Jacob and through the deepest holy of holies. This is not a path to a celestial home, but how we can attain a connection to it. To open our eyes to see the divine heaven here on earth and live in that glory rather than pine away for it. These ideas are layered into the allegories and symbols that Freemasonry promulgates today from a vestige of meaning from the past. So too, is this our link to the ancient mystery schools in spirit if not in the flesh.

From the Ziggurats of Ur to the Egyptian mysteries, the breadth of Hinduism and the creation of the Torah, the school of Pythagoras, the Hermetic traditions, the Evolution of Christianity and later Islam, the Kabbalah traditions to the Christian mysticism and unfoldment of the self in the new age and in modern psychology, each of these ideas evolving through time to later merge and meld with a Rosicrucian alchemy whose roots go back to the Roman Empire and passed from one seeker to another, one esoteric group to another, to eventually be taken in by the societies sub rosas and emerge in the hands of the Free-stone masons and practiced in lodge. This tradition has moved into and through the world esoteric schools, knowingly and unknowingly, each proclaiming lineage, but equally with few credentials to show historically. What we are left with are the pieces of our "secret" existence to proclaim our lineage to the vestiges of a mythic past. But this unlikely list of thoughts connects subconsciously with mans universal quest for those unanswered questions of the unknown, establishing the principal of this Mystery School tradition and the basis of esoteric study.

We know that these schools existed to communicate these ideas and to teach those willing to learn them. Subconsciously, part of their purpose was to carry on those traditions for future generations in their texts and traditions so future generations could rediscover them and use them to act as future beacons of learning. Their education is not whole and concrete, but remains an intangible and abstract of questions from whose answers demand we continue to ask through our generations.

Many Masons reject this connection of esotericism and see only an institute that caters to the community aspect, basing the fraternity on their own personal faiths and choosing not to see its associations with other seekers. This is not a fault, but instead another turn on the wheel of the traditions cycle of development. In the Rosicrucian tradition, its adherents were instructed to live as those whose land they reside, worshiping as they do and this, subconsciously, may be what is taking place by applying letter to law. But I believe that the true nature of Freemasonry at its core exists in both realms, a balance of fraternity and ceremonial initiation of letter and law whose value is in the creation of its shared experience. From it we can delve into this esoteric past from whence we came and explore the ideas of our generations and shape them in our time for how the future will study them. Where knowledge of them is enough to give them life and encourage the exploration of these esoteric mysteries.

# VI

## EDUCATION, LIGHT AND WHERE IT'S HIDDEN

All men who have undertaken the trials of their Masonic degrees are charged to seek one thing earnestly, and that is more light in Masonry. Masonic Light, I have found, is a wide field of research and study. Whether it's history, religion, belief, rituals, or symbols, the study can traverse through all of these areas often blending and blurring between them. And interestingly, it does not exist in a vacuum, but in an environment where there are many other people doing research and studying, who have very likely raised these same questions, topics and ideas.

It has been said that there is more research and books on the topic of "Freemasonry" than on any other subject, which I have found to be believable at times but far from true. But, with the myriad of Research lodges, societies, and clubs, its history is still in a relative eclipse as we delve deeper to find links to our philosophical underpinnings so prevalent in the degrees we practice.

Many research lodges who have functioned as these scribes and historians then have dedicated themselves solely to the study and research of various aspects of the Fraternity, acting as a principal source to bridge the volumes of Masonic scholarship to the legions of members. But how much of the knowledge has permeated the public mind? Has it re-entered the moral imagination of society at large? Or has it re-entered a growing public sphere where little interaction in the last half century has allowed its name to become the fodder for countless conspiracies and fictions about its rites and rituals? The organization itself, sequestering the history, has instead focused more on charity than its progressive philosophy.

In more recent history, as the occasional film comes out, National Treasure, the Di Vinci Code and others the fraternity garners some mention but none seem to capture the essence of the craft, only using it as a plot point to further the story. Perhaps it is that Freemasonry is not really a "thing" as such, but instead the essence, ethereal and intangible. It is not necessarily a cause of an action but a contributor, the unseen impetus of our existence.

With that in mind then, is Freemasonry a thing? Is it a tangible substance or a material object? Or is it just an idea embodied by the men who join, with its very foundation laying claim to its permanence, when in reality it is as fluid as society itself in its composition. Does that give it a substance? By people working the craft, is that enough to make it tangible, or will it forever live within the realm of the ideal?

One thing I have discovered is that "Masonic Light" does not emanate from one source. Instead, I perceive it coming from a variety of sources; often from places you would least expect it. Directly, I see Masonic light coming from within. We each carry the light, learning from its reflection on the things we illuminate with our wisdom. The most profound and illuminating of sources is through the interaction of brothers both in and out of lodge. Ironically, I feel that it is not just Freemason Brothers, but all seekers of light and higher illumination.

Like the bejeweled night sky, spanning horizon to horizon.

The illumination we seek is an internal understanding of our relationship to the divine and I would argue that all light leads to the same divinity though known by different names in different lands. Freemasonry is but one path to that end. It not being a faith, it is rather a way to conceive the divine, a way to conceive God. Once understood, the light that is believed illusive becomes apparent and is found to reside within, and we shine it upon all that we see, knowledge being that fount from which the aspirant drinks from to fuel that light to shine into the darkness.

Few of us can imagine finding this, until it becomes evident in our work and only then does it become the beauty imagined.

# VII
## DO OUR OATHS
## MATTER?

I believe in convergence. The kind of convergence when things come together in obscure and often unforeseen ways and create a previously unseen third path or solution. This convergence experience came to me in the form of a question about how to initiate a Islamist candidate into Freemasonry with the Koran as the Holy Book, and suitable passages to correlate with the three degrees. After talking to some brothers, and considering the situation, a very intelligent brother who is himself a Muslim, and wise in the ways of the fraternity finally aided me to find an equitable solution to the question.

But the resulting convergence came to me when at the same time as the question was posed, I ran across a recent op-ed article that was on why the Holy Bible should be the ONLY Holy Book an American elected leader should ever swear their oaths of affirmation for truth and faithful public service on. The argument was that as the American civilization was founded on the basis of the Christian Bible, the oaths of public office should affirm to that foundational belief and should not allow any other sacred text be used to swear their oath.

The convergence came to me in making that same claim within in Freemasonry. The question that arose was "do some within the membership see the fraternity as strictly a Judeo Christian institution, closed to recognizing the wealth of other faiths that exist within the world"? And more so, that as individuals come into the fold do their faiths (or sacred writings) deserve a place on just an equal footing as the bible.

It should be said that many jurisdictions and Grand Lodges recognize many sacred laws and do give them a prominent place for the oaths in many instances allowing the book to sit atop the same alter so that both are venerated for their wisdom traditions. But few American Grand Lodges directly replace outright the bible with these other books, on the presumption that American masonry was predicated on this book in particular as the great light of wisdom.

I can say that in earlier times, including the era of America's foundation, the fraternity's obvious external influence was Christianity, lacking the beautiful diversity it does today. Different "faiths" were looked at as different where religious freedom more often referred to decisions between protestant denominations. Even at the time America broke in away from the English monarchy, kingdoms were believed affirmed by divine Christian edict. It was the Christian God who made kingdoms, not men. But were the ideas inherent in the Constitution really echo's of the Judeo-Christian Bible, or affirmations in the divine nature of man to rule himself? Even the idea itself of religious Freedom evolved to include all faiths and not one in particular.

With the asking of the question, it made me wonder: "is this the zeitgeist of the nation"? "Does our religious freedom only pertain to choice in Christian ethos or is it broader than that narrow conception"? In our country of religious freedoms do we only see the many denominations of the Holy Bible as the founding testament upon which to proclaim our honesty and fidelity? Is that our religious freedom?

The tradition of swearing oaths is a long one and in this particular instance it can be traced back to our American founding fathers where the original swearing in ceremony of President George Washington started an institution borrowing from the traditions in Freemasonry, insofar as to use the bible from Saint John's Lodge, No 1, in New York for the ceremony. But was this act a foundation of a specific tradition, or just the representation of binding ones faith on a book they hold holy?

This convergence made me start to wonder about our Masonic oaths. The question that came to mind was "is the holy book dependant upon the oath takers faith or will any sacred texts suffice"? Does making someone swear an oath on something they do not see as sacred make their allegiance any less binding? Or is it merely symbolic to the institution that is the supposed foundation stone of morality?

Washington's oath on the bible solidified the monumental founding of America from its preceding centuries establishment on Divine placement, so is that reason enough to establish a principal reason for the future? Even a deist, with a remote conception of God, still has faith. Freemasonry, I feel, illuminates the way here of actively engaging a petitioners belief system, by fashioning our initiations accordingly. The choice of holy books then represents its purpose, to sanctify and add gravity to the very act of taking the oath. It is not to make a candidate more comfortable, but to impress upon them that there own sacred oath is backed up by their sacred faith which then act subconsciously with what they hold to be inviolate, essentially to what they hold as divine.

This convergence for me carried with it a two fold meaning:

that not only is it relevant in discussion but in the more importance value of the very obligation itself. It raised the question facing lodges in this increasingly religious diversified world, in similar fashion to the way in which our very own government is facing this change.

Understanding this creates a wider more and more diverse understanding of that realm of the sacred. That the idea of God does not just exist in one conception; it instead resides in all of us and in all of our myriad faiths and faith teachings. With that in mind and our own individual beliefs at bay, is any one faith greater than the other? Remember there is a divine spark in man that bears a close resemblance to the supreme intelligence of the universe. In a situation where men meet upon the level and in a faith neutral environment, should one text be held above another? How could we not see the value in all faiths?

# VIII

# FREEMASONRY, THE RELIGION OF NOT BEING A RELIGION

A prevalent criticism of Freemasonry in the 20th Century is that the ancient Fraternity is a religion. That in its teachings it espouses the ethos of a new belief as a hybrid of Judeo/Christian resurrection and salvation in its rites and practices. Often, these charges come on the calls from many specific evangelical sources that have tied the notion of religion and faith together into a hybrid of idea and action that is uniquely their own as it conforms to their faith practice. They see "Religion and faith" as a singular idea and inseparable, and as such they demonize the practices of ideas and rituals that venerate the existence of a sovereign supreme being as an affront to their own unique idea of how things "should" be done. The charge levied, is that Freemasonry is a religion, and as such it is an abomination to their way of thinking about their faith practice issuing a prohibition to its members from becoming one. Essentially, they say it is an affront to their deity, forgetting that in the country that they call home, there is an open toleration for all faiths and religious practices.

All of this leads to the question: "Is Freemasonry a religion"?

Perhaps a better way to phrase this question would be is Freemasonry is a faith practice. More broadly does the activity of Freemasonry constitute the summation that it is the promulgation of a belief system and a replacement of all other systems?

The quick observational answer is no, Freemasonry is not a religion, in that it does not teach FAITH. It does, however, strive to bring a philosophical and allegorical set of ideas about the divine forward and, in that sense could be construed as one which requires the observer to separate the two from one another. Faith as separate from Religion.

From the Webster's definition of **Religion** it is:
1. A set of beliefs concerning the cause, nature, and purpose of the universe, esp. when considered as the creation of a superhuman agency or agencies, usually involving devotional and ritual observances, and often containing a moral code governing the conduct of human affairs.
2. A specific fundamental set of beliefs and practices generally agreed upon by a number of persons or sects: the Christian religion; the Buddhist religion.
3. The body of persons adhering to a particular set of beliefs and practices: a world council of religions.
4. The life or state of a monk, nun, etc.: to enter religion.
5. The practice of religious beliefs; ritual observance of faith.
6. Something one believes in and follows devotedly; a point or matter of ethics or conscience: to make a religion of fighting prejudice.
7. Religions, Archaic. Religious rites.
8. Archaic. strict faithfulness; devotion: a religion to one's vow
—Idiom
9. Get religion, Informal. a. To acquire a deep conviction of the validity of religious beliefs and practices. b. To resolve to mend one's errant ways: The company got religion and stopped making

dangerous products.

Origin: 1150–1200; ME religioun.

This is NOT wholly faith, though the two share some defining terms.

From the same dictionary the definition of **Faith** is:

1. Confidence or trust in a person or thing: faith in another's ability.

2. Belief that is not based on proof: He had faith that the hypothesis would be substantiated by fact.

3. Belief in God or in the doctrines or teachings of religion: the firm faith of the Pilgrims.

4. Belief in anything, as a code of ethics, standards of merit, etc.: to be of the same faith with someone concerning honesty.

5. System of religious belief: the Christian faith; the Jewish faith.

6. The obligation of loyalty or fidelity to a person, promise, engagement, etc.: Failure to appear would be breaking faith.  a. The observance of this obligation; fidelity to one's promise, oath, allegiance, etc.: He was the only one who proved his faith during our recent troubles.

7. Christian Theology. The trust in God and in His promises as made through Christ and the Scriptures by which humans are justified or saved.

Freemasonry does not proclaim a belief not based on proof. It is a system of ethics, but then so are the Boy Scouts. It does proclaim a confidence in a person, the candidate who is forming his ashlar. But it does not imply a belief, in a specific agent of belief. Rather, its Rites directly demand the participant to have his faith as his own..

But we must note the difference in word origins, religion comes from the Latin root meaning to tie, fasten, bind. Faith's origin is to trust.

The difference here is that in all of the writings in the past they refer to Freemasonry in some way as a "religion" NOT as a faith. The problem today is that the fundamental argument that Freemasonry is a religion confuses the two definitions to mean exactly the same thing and presumes that any religion must also be a faith. The difference here being that assumption is false and the two are not dependent on one another.

Albert Pike, the oft-quoted villain of the "Masonic Religion" detractors does say that Freemasonry is perhaps a representation of all religion in a passage from the 10th degree of Scottish rite Masonry saying[1]:

*Masonry is not a religion. He who makes of it a religious belief, falsifies and denaturalizes it. The Brahmin, the Jew, the Mahometan, the Catholic, the Protestant, each professing his peculiar religion, sanctioned by the laws, by time, and by climate, must needs retain it, and cannot have two religions; for the social and sacred laws adapted to the usages, manners, and prejudices of particular countries, are the work of men.*

But Masonry teaches, and has preserved in their purity, the cardinal tenets of the old primitive faith, which underlie and are the foundation of all religions. All that ever existed have had a basis of truth; and all have overlaid that truth with errors. The primitive truths taught by the Redeemer were sooner corrupted, and intermingled and alloyed with fictions than when taught to the first of our race. Masonry is the universal morality which is suitable to the inhabitants of every clime, to the man of every creed. It has taught no doctrines, except those truths that tend directly to the well-being of man; and those who have attempted to direct it toward useless vengeance, political ends, and Jesuitism, have merely perverted it to purposes foreign to its pure spirit and real nature.

I suggest that Pike backs this up by saying on p.160, that the key is toleration, and without it, it becomes an argument without merit or conclusion over who is more right than the others.

Pike saying further:

*Toleration, holding that every other man has the same right to his opinion and faith that we have to ours; and liberality, holding that as no human being can with certainty say, in the clash and conflict of hostile faiths and creeds, what is truth, or that he is surely in possession of it, so every one should feel that it is quite possible that another equally honest and sincere with himself, and yet holding the contrary opinion, may himself be in possession of the truth, and that whatever one firmly and conscientiously believes, is truth, to him--these are the mortal enemies of that fanaticism which persecutes for opinion's sake, and initiates crusades against whatever it, in its imaginary holiness, deems to be contrary to the law of God or verity of dogma. And education, instruction, and enlightenment are the most certain means by which fanaticism and intolerance can be rendered powerless.*

With these quotes in mind is Freemasonry a faith? No, not at all. Is Freemasonry a Religion? Perhaps in its practice, yes, as it carries forward a tradition from the past to be taught to generations in the future, but not a dogmatic belief system with specifics to salvation. Is Freemasonry tolerant of all faiths? Yes. Does that frighten, distance, and otherwise disenfranchise all fundamental ideologues? Yes, it does, which is why every organized dogmatically proscribed faith denounces Freemasonry.

Freemasonry is the religion of not being a religion, the faith of all faiths. It says that no one faith is right, and no one faith is wrong, which is diametrically opposed to what any fundamentalist body wants to tell you is right.

But let's look to the original constitutions by Anderson, written in 1723 to the creation of the first codified constitutions of Freemasonry. He says:

### I. Concerning GOD and RELIGION.

*A Mason is oblig'd by his Tenure, to obey the moral law; and if he rightly understands the Art, he will never be a stupid Atheist nor an irreligious Libertine. But though in ancient Times Masons were charg'd in every Country to be of the Religion of that Country or Nation, whatever it was, yet 'tis now thought more expedient only to oblige them to that Religion in which all Men agree, leaving their particular Opinions to themselves; that is, to be good Men and true, or Men of Honour and Honesty, by whatever Denominations or Persuasions they may be distinguish'd; whereby Masonry becomes the Center of Union, and the Means of conciliating true Friendship among Persons that must have remain'd at a perpetual Distance.*

In this short passage, there is no mention of how to worship or create a deity, nor is there a charge to manifest a belief in some unknown conception. What it does suggest is that in all religions there is a basis of universality, some spark of common denominator, and it is to that essence that all men reverently believe. It is from this that most anti-Masons take their cue, that to recognize any other deity is blasphemous and heretical to their conception of faith, but this alienates and demands compliance to believe what others say is right.

A mistake in understanding here is that it is not a appropriation of something Christian, no more than virginal birth was taken from the Mithraism tradition. Neither is it a "mimicking or mockery" to conduct a rite or ritual that venerates deity through operations of men beneath the canopy of the divines heavens. Rather, it is recognizing the act and its universality towards all faith traditions, which puts it at odds with their own theological practice.

In the end, Pike is just an interpreter of the tradition, and writes his analysis of the degrees of Scottish Rite Masonry, which are allegorical plays to convey these teachings. The allegory in this degree speaks to the universal connection between past master, and ultimately all mankind, including Abraham, Moses, Jesus, and so on. With that emphasis, the point isn't dead masters, as you say, but that we have those past masters within us, that their energy and ideas are mingled with our own.

This is a difficult idea to understand, and more difficult to accept, but the Western religious tradition has separated our connectivity with the divine and externalized it to be a force removed from us. What Pikes talks about in much of his analysis is an internalizing of faith, something found more in Hermetic traditions, or the mystery traditions. Some have said it resembles the Gnostic teachings of early Christendom

A theme I take away is the search for the mystical experience and the concern of evangelized theology. One of the aspects I have found in Freemasonry is that it is like a religion, but not a faith. The practice is liturgical and the catechism is universally teaching a message, but the message is not on divinity, or on faith. It is, the religion of not being a religion. It is a difficult concept, as there is nothing else to compare it to, as no other system promotes faith without saying in who that faith resides, which is how we come to the idea of the Great Architect. In this embodiment, we can collect all ideas of the divine as the creation of the universe, the Monad, or the point of creation.

Experience trumps once removed opinion. Some quote from the detractors of Freemasonry, but few actually have been Masons, and of those who have, fabricate and lie to bolster their individual agenda such as Jim Shaw[2] and Leo Taxili[3].

The craft lodge teaches (as do the Rites) a more universalistic approach to believers. It neither promotes nor denounces any one faith, even with its leaning towards a more Christian identity. The system today is a vestige of the age in which it was devised. Much of what Freemasonry teaches comes from its past connection to Hermetica, in almost an equal measure with Kabala, the Old Testament, and Christian mysticism. It is from these sources that it attempts to draw out its parables and mythology. Pike, in his work, organized and codified much into the 32 degrees, not as religious absolutes, but as important paths of the mystical, to achieve that connection we seek within to the divine.

The latter is what I think many evangelical Christians take umbrage with and deride Freemasonry about, because is it not their specific path of faith, that it represents a "different" path. Even quoting the biblical "…no other path to me…" grounds the argument in a "my belief is right" and closes out any that challenge that assertion. Even a Christian is allowed some degree of latitude in what they believe, especially as the bible was written by others and not Jesus. It is faith that should guide us and not the religion that codifies its adherence. If it were otherwise, why would the protestant reformation even of taken place?

It is in this lack of a dominating opinion of how the practice should be conducted where we find the most infuriating issue. Because of the open stance of the Fraternity and the willingness that it has as being an ecumenical and non sectarian practice, it puts all faiths on an equal footing, not allowing any one faith to leverage power or authority over another. It does raise the question of whether this was the original intent of Anderson when he wrote the original constitutions in 1723, but even in that time there were struggles to between Catholic and Protestant control in England. Where better plant the seeds of unity than in a system that openly accepts men of all faiths and a charge to meet them all on the same level to traverse a third way. It is here that we can find the religion of not being a religion, and with our faith in the divine work to build our world for all mankind.

# IX

# FREEMASONRY IN MODERN ART

Many Masonic brethren may not realize, but Freemasonry has made its way into modern art carrying much of its symbolism into the modern pop culture, while leaving behind much of its meaning. Specifically recognized by their characteristic Red fez's and jackets, the Shriners are today portrayed as mid-century (1950's) party animals, often caught in the act of their fun.

The artist Josh "Shag" Agle has utilized the iconography of the Noble Shrine in weaving them into characters from the 50's while captivating vivid moments of their cultural notoriety (or infamy) in a social landscape.[1] In his work, we see these mid century revelers as Tiki Lounge devotees at the height of martini sipping frivolity their memory in time focusing on their entertainments rather than their works.

In these descriptions, Shag commentary is not about fraternity, or brotherly love, no, it is of graphic depictions of rampant consumerism and consumption, which is the result of their activities. The iconographic Shriner partying and cavorting in their crimson

Wives , Image courtesy of Shag. © 2000, 2010 Josh Agle

regalia doing what they so notably once did, party.

It is no hidden secret, nor is it a skeleton in the closet, that Shrine conventions have always been an illustrious to-do. Even the singer song writer Ray Stevens[2] has depicted their late century cavorting as something of legend when the Shriners come to town. But another such example is a story dating back to 1937 where in Detroit an army of 100,000 converged on the city for a 3 day convention to elect an imperial potentate.

Heavy Drinkers, Image courtesy of Shag. © 2000, 2010 Josh Agle

Undoubtedly, this seems to of become part of the collective remembrance of society that Shriners party. Has this impacted the shifting conservative mind of the American public? Did the Baby Boom generation grow up hearing stories about these parties, and collectively log them as something our Grandparents did, so it's not for me. Maybe it's a good thing, the distance that the Shrine has made to the rest of the Fraternity.

This same iconography is portrayed in a music video for the song Blood and Thunder, by the band Mastodon[3]. The red fez, the saber and crescent, even the partying clowns are all images that have carried over from the past into the modern culture.

Mr. X, Image courtesy of Shag. © 2000, 2010 Josh Agle

It really seems that there was a place in the world for these things, at that time and that as society was more external and open to a sense of social civil society, these activities were more commonplace. But as we have shifted towards a more selfish and isolated consumption filled world the editorial message in Shag's paintings and Mastodon's video's become more a commentary on how we as a society have fallen into a pattern of greater consumerism today. Remember, there were no Wal-Marts in the 1950's, at least not in the way they appear today, and that a disposable wasteful society was looked down upon. Perhaps this is a good indication of why things are the way they are today. Did we begin to simply consume too much? Did we begin to consume ourselves?

# X
# LOSS OF SYMBOLIC MEANING

The knowledge of symbolism is lost today in a sea of symbolic overload. At every turn a milieu of symbols look back at us broadcasting their own individual idea. The messages are as varied as the symbols themselves: buy me, support me, follow me, play me, watch me, identify with me, all so overwhelming that we ourselves can become personally identified by the series of symbols that we wear which visually describe who we are. This becomes, in effect, our own cultural identity.

So what does that mean to Freemasonry? As a personal education system of symbols and allegories, we stand in competition with a world of full of symbolic meaning. This has not always been the problem, as there were less significant visual competition. But over time, mans ability to learn through the understanding of symbols has become dulled with the visual noise created from the profusion of modern symbolic messages. What this creates is an overlap of symbolic imagery competing to communicate their unique message.

This change in symbolic distribution changed our individual understanding. We took the symbols to their external correlations and not their internal meaning. This is not to say that every simple shape of collection of objects means something specific, but certain symbols evoke a message not easily understood by those capable of distilling their meaning. These meanings, however, are not to be understood externally; rather they are meant to be replayed to form an internal understanding, to become ingrained on the subconscious level to form identity.

In times past, the education of the mystery schools channeled this education through very few outlets, and with a stronger more salient message, delivered to entice people more to explore its message. But, as what happens with evolution, time and environment have changed and Freemasonry has not. Our symbols today speak to an era long gone by and have become lost to the uninitiated on their meaning, purpose, and importance which has been drown by an overload of icons. The studies of these internal symbols are quickly becoming relegated to a modern history that is forgetting its near past, by ignoring its archaic origins, and decrying its ideals. Ironically, they are the very ideas that are in even more need today.

The symbols of Freemasonry, even to Freemasons, are no longer studied seriously, and are instead diverted to monitors and auxiliary classes more easily ignored by the membership at large. Freemasonry itself is responsible for this dilution of its symbolic significance. The symbols and meanings that were once experienced at every meeting needs to be reintroduced to the membership as symbolic to what Freemasonry is, and what Freemasons are expected to be. The modes of communicating the meaning of the symbols may vary whether through public service (charity), open houses, public awareness, campaigns, family outreach, lodge discussion, symbolism classes, or meeting discussion, all of which require involvement. The symbols of Freemasonry are powerful, as any master who has contemplated their meaning will attest, but powerful symbolism is worthless if not studied or taught properly about their meaning. This does not mean to advertise them as a commodity, instead we need to show by example their value and worth. Only then will the symbols of Freemasonry have a chance to be more visible again through the overwhelming sea of symbolism.

Within Masonic circles, it is said few ever studied Masonic symbolism, that it became evident only to those inclined to see it. But I do not believe this to be true. Freemasonry has always been a system of symbols, delivered to an audience on a manner to being interpreted and studied. This system was established as a progressive system of symbol, so on or off the path of enlightenment to ignore that is ignoring the foundation of our whole system of symbolic meaning.

# XI

# HERMETIC
# TRADITION AND
# AMERICA

*The following ideas coalesced following a lecture given by Dr. Stephen Hoeller,*
*Regionary Bishop of Ecclesia Gnostica, on the same subject in 2007.*

How many of us understand what Hermetic thought is, beyond the idea of "hermetically sealed"? For those unaware, the Hermetic tradition is an esoteric vein of study based on texts, believed to of originated in Egypt, near or about the time when Christ was born. The basis of hermetic thought is that of a providential deity whose strongest commandment was to "do no evil" and that the notion of the divine is as infinite as imaginable.

The idea of a Hermetic American Republic essentially is that the ideas and efforts of the founding fathers were the results of a broader sub current of the intelligentsia within society, whose ideas manifested themselves into the early ideas, concepts and documents and foundation of the American Republic.

To talk about this though, we need to understand where this idea of Hermetica came from. The roots of Hermetica are traceable to roughly 300 B.C.E., as its is believed to have started as an Egyptian tradition based on the Egyptian god Thoth, the god of the moon and night was also associated with messages and communication, principally between the deities of the day. The Thoth connection becomes diluted as a follower of Thoth calls his god *megistou kai megistou theou megalou Hermou*[1], which is the earliest surviving form of his mention as a *"three times great god"*. Later Greek translations will attribute the Egyptian god Thoth to the Greek Hermes, that suggests Thoth/Hermes to of been the scribe who etched ancient stile and whose second incarnation wrote into books the teachings of Hermetica around 4 B.C.E.[2]  At that time there were many texts attributed to Hermes/Trismegistos which were translated into Greek as examples of ancient Egyptian wisdom.

These "wisdoms" were brought forward by early Christian scholars who attributed their accuracy to their theology placing them in truth with their Christian doctrines. They were studied for many years as mystery texts that supported the tenants of Christian theology.

At some point, these texts and ideas became encapsulated thoughts of Hermetic wisdom and were attributed to the magus Hermes Trismegistos that we look to from the period of the early Renaissance.

Thoth as the Egyptian god of the moon and the night associated with messages and writing, was represented in Egypt under the form of the ibis. It is from this nature the god Thoth was said to be of wisdom, which may be a hidden key to its relationship with Freemasonry.  It is thought that Hermetica flourished in ancient Alexandria amongst many other philosophies, but moved underground and fell out of common knowledge with the fall of Rome and the onset of the Middle Ages.

Tobias Churton suggests that these ideas flowed into the Arabic/Islamic world and into the practice of Sufi's who related the teachings to a broad concept of God, rather than the dogmatic one of the Koran.[3]

With the Renaissance came a resurgence of interest in knowledge, including the rediscovery of the Hermetic texts. Believed brought to Europe by the Medici family from sources in Byzantium, these texts contained now ancient threads of wisdom that talked in detail about a dual nature to man, the goodness of the divine, and the infiniteness of deity, and mans pursuit to unify man to the divine. Man, it says is, made up of a human lower self that includes feelings, thoughts, sensation, and ego, the human traits we recognize today. The other half consisted of the spirit, that intangible, ineffable thing that gives us that higher conscience. The Hermetic "texts" cultivated the idea of the conscious coming together in the initiates self with his spirit. To join the two, the transformation of these elements separate elements into a wholly new one. Some believe that Hermetic tradition survived the fall of Rome and the middle ages in the ideas of alchemy, which has existed in various forms over centuries.

With the blossoming Renaissance, Hermetic thought began to weave itself into Christian mythos which was quickly stamped out by the doctrinal inquisition which rejected the philosophical ideation of a personal God consciousness. Some examples of this sanitization of this transformative self-consciousness can be seen in the extermination of both the Templar's and Cather's in France. They were by no means the only example of this purge, but are perhaps the clearest and most recognized. Suggesting this creates a paradox of conspiracy against occultism that there was a contentious program to eradicate this thought, but truthfully I doubt this was the case. Instead over years, as one dogmatic program preceded another, each took its successive step in consolidating its power, eradicating its opposition. Much the way Gnosticism was pushed to the fringes of Christian theology in the early years before the Nicean formation of Catholicism. But again, the ideas did not die, nor were they completely eradicated. The Hermeticists moved in their circles underground into the "secret societies" whose aegis was to continue, like the symbol of Thoth, the communication of his knowledge, not fully knowing its origin nor its importance as an alternative to what was otherwise the state understanding of religion. Two such societies that appeared from this underground were the Rosicrucian's and Freemasonry.

Within Freemasonry the attributes of Hermetic study was evident by a series of steps, or degrees, where the initiated would learn different aspects of the knowledge slowly to cultivate the eventual merger into the self. These steps patterned in with the mystical exploration of alchemy and into the science of the cathedral builders whose traditions had for centuries folded into the sacred geometry used to build the houses of God. Ultimately, these degrees would come to symbolize the physical and mental awakening of the individual God consciousness, epitomized in the phrase "Know Thyself".

This unconscious cognition moved though Europe ultimately finding a receptive home in England where it was incubated and nurtured amidst revolution and religious freedom, away from the Catholic Church.

These ideas, most likely unintentionally, found their way into the foundations of America.

Like the establishment of that city on a hill, as pulled from Matthew[4] and proclaimed by John Smith at the founding of the first American settlements, this idea was distinctly Christian, but had also been cultivated in the private societies of the preceding centuries, as illuminated by Francis Bacon's New Atlantis. This text, published in

1626, likely made its way into the subconscious of the Puritans and later settlers, but by the time the fabric of America was starting to weave together, the ideas of a sovereign man became directly connected with our constitution, which is a direct contextual connection to the ancient Hermetic thought. One example of this connection is the inherent separation of Church and State as Hermetic tradition tells us that each individual chooses his path to their own understanding of the divine, and should not be directed or influenced one way or another. Freedom of religion is a direct extension of this idea, and manifests this principal in the ethos that the state is the vessel of the people and should not dictate one faith by presuming authority of one or another. The initiate must find his self and not be told where or what he is.

Public education is a step in this extension of the Hermetic philosophy too, through the exploration of the physical universe around us. How does one attain sufficient knowledge to reach consciousness except by learning about their physical universe to its most distant horizon? Knowledge, or gnosis, creates a divine metal (alchemically referred to as mercury) of the body giving it its strength and resiliency. This freedom of knowledge makes awareness attainable to all who desire it and subsequently creating a better person and citizen.

Lastly, the three branches of government working in an imperfect conjunction of opposites creating a balance of good of the body, the ultimate attainment of the self. Balance democracy owing its heritage in part to this Hermetic tradition. Our forefather, the pantheon of America's nation builders, has some of these ideas form by living in the country, but many belonged to societies that practiced these traditions. Democracy, self knowledge through progressive degrees of understanding and a separation of a controlled theology were all tenants of Freemasonry which was the inheritor of this sacred Hermetic philosophy.

Today, this tradition may seem antiquated and even superfluous, but it is the model of our origin and a shining example of the progress towards that city upon the hill. History may consider the secret societies as below the sight of the mainstream, but it was not the membership that passed itself on through the ages, but rather the ancient communication of the development of the self, the vestige of Thoth and the Thrice great Hermes, as the message brought forward to us today. It is that message of self discovery that is transferred to us, as we become the inheritors of its memory to be re-communicated to the future.

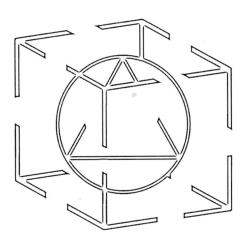

# XII

# FREEMASONRY AND THE KYBALION

*Seven Principals in*
*Three Degrees*

Freemasonry is often attributed to the ideas of Hermetica, or more specifically to Hermetic principals. With that in mind, I felt it would be good to talk about one of the key modern hermetic texts and explore some of the obvious parallels we can find in them to the degrees of craft Freemasonry. In that discussion I believe we can pull from it some conclusions and make some philosophical connections to create and application between the two. In doing so, we can make practical the degrees towards this Hermetic principal.

As reference, the source text used here is *"The Kybalion"* originally published in 1908 by the "three initiates". It is suggested that it is the work of Paul Foster Case, the founder of the *Builders of the Adytum*[1], and brother Master Mason, as well as the writer and publisher on the early new age and New Thought movements William Walker Atkinson, and one of the early founders of the *Golden Dawn* Michael Whitty.

Each of the people and groups mentioned may seem disconnected from what we see as Modern Freemasonry, when in fact there contributions came at a time when there were many such groups delving towards a deeper understanding of the traditions that Freemasonry brought forth.

For a more academic look at Hermetics, I recommend the reader to explore *Hermetica* by Copenhaver. Though the texts differ, Hermetica is said to be the original source material for alchemy and hermetic knowledge from the Middle Ages and Renaissance philosophy, from which Masonry blossomed.

To understand the text we must first look at the history of the philosophy as it was written in the Kybalion. This text attributes its origins to the original writings of Hermes Triesmegustus, who is suggested as the scribe of the Gods and who dwelt in ancient Egypt. It is also suggested that he was a contemporary of Abraham, in biblical history. It is to Hermes that all western esoteric teaching is said to have originated, in that through this philosophy, Hermes planted the "great seed of truth" instead of founding a teaching school as many other great philosophers of his age did. It was by mouth to ear communication that his wisdom was passed through the ages. But also it was cautioned that it is not for everyone in that the lips (words or wisdom) are closed, except to those with the ears of understanding. To preserve the wisdom, the ancient teachers warned against allowing the secret doctrine to become crystallized into a creed which would allow it to become dogmatic and inflexible.

Instead, it was "...*passed along from master to student from initiate to Hierophant. When it was written down, it was veiled in terms of alchemy and astrology, so that only he that posses the key could read it aright...*" "*The Hermetic Philosophy is the only master key which will open all the doors of the occult teachings!*"

Much of this history is fanciful and well imagined, but the Hermetic teachings have been linked to a late period of Egypt, and like most ancient or religious in nature texts their true origin and history is in shadow. It is from this tradition that it is supposed that Freemasonry originated. As a continuation of the Egyptian mystery schools, the method of teaching, and the philosophy taught was promulgated forward. Perhaps of significance is the point of preventing the philosophy from becoming dogmatic or crystallized into a specific creed. But even faced with that question, the philosophy has at various points been studied and adopted as an aspect of other faiths, including Christianity and Judaism. And it is in this connection that we can draw parallels to Gnosticism, which was in a sense a middle way between them. For this discussion however we do need to consider one aspect of Gnosticism as its early conception of knowledge (gnosis) and the residence of the divine as an internal agent rather than an external one, which we can find in our reading of Hermetica.

With this brief history, we can now look at the seven applied Hermetic principals from the Kybalion which are:

THE PRINCIPLE OF MENTALISM.
THE PRINCIPLE OF CORRESPONDENCE.
THE PRINCIPLE OF VIBRATION.
THE PRINCIPLE OF POLARITY.
THE PRINCIPLE OF RHYTHM.
THE PRINCIPLE OF CAUSE AND EFFECT.
THE PRINCIPLE OF GENDER.

These Seven Principles will be the core of this analysis as we proceed ahead. The purpose here is to examine each of the principals of the Kybalion and find their connection points within Freemasonry.

# THE PRINCIPLE OF MENTALISM

"THE ALL IS MIND; The Universe is Mental."
*-The Kybalion*

This Principle embodies the truth that "All is Mind." It explains that *THE ALL (which is the Substantial Reality underlying all the outward manifestations and appearances which we know under the terms of "The Material Universe"; the "Phenomena of Life"; "Matter"; "Energy"; and, in short, all that is apparent to our material senses) is SPIRIT which in itself is UNKNOWABLE and UNDEFINABLE, but which may be considered and thought of as AN UNIVERSAL, INFINITE, LIVING MIND. It also explains that all the phenomenal world or universe is simply a Mental Creation of THE ALL, subject to the Laws of Created Things, and that the universe, as a whole, and in its parts or units, has its existence in the Mind of THE ALL, in which Mind we "live and move and have our being."* This Principle, by establishing the Mental Nature of the Universe, easily explains all of the varied mental and psychic phenomena that occupy such a large portion of the public attention, and which, without such explanation, are non-understandable and defy scientific treatment. An understanding of this great Hermetic Principle of Mentalism enables the individual to readily grasp the laws of the Mental Universe, and to apply the same to his well-being and advancement. *The Hermetic Student is enabled to apply intelligently the great Mental Laws, instead of using them in a haphazard manner. With the Master-Key in his possession, the student may unlock the many doors of the mental and psychic temple of knowledge, and enter the same freely and intelligently.* This Principle explains the true nature of "Energy," "Power," and "Matter," and why and how all these are subordinate to the Mastery of Mind. One of the old Hermetic Masters wrote, long ages ago: "He who grasps the truth of the Mental Nature of the Universe is well advanced on The Path to Mastery." And these words are as true today as at the time they were first written. Without this Master-Key, Mastery is impossible, and the student knocks in vain at the many doors of The Temple.

-*The Kybalion*

At first glance it is difficult to see anything that would seem to link itself to Freemasonry. But in close examination and some extrapolation we can formulate some links to help associate the idea of MENTALISM into some of the precepts in Masonry.

First in the term of the "Substantial Reality" which we call the Material universe, we can get a sense this expansive term is as the "Great Architect" as more than an individual or person, but as this text identifies it as "a spirit" which is in itself unknowable and indefinable, perhaps even ineffable.

This notion of the ineffable seems to change the construct of an external divine agent into a greater mental agent, suggesting that the universe is a creation of the all (God or monad) mind and that as it is extended to the created, we create through this same mental power. Not a tangible creation, something from nothing, but by making manifest those things we apply our mind to. The very act of creation. This is an aspect of this mentalism.

This we can see as the Kybalion suggests, "*The Hermetic Student is enabled to apply intelligently the great Mental Laws, instead of using them in a haphazard manner. With the Master-Key in his possession* [mentalism], *the student may unlock the many doors of the mental and psychic temple of knowledge, and enter the same freely and intelligently. This Principle explains the true nature of "Energy," "Power," and "Matter," and why and how all these are subordinate to the Mastery of Mind."* In this process we can see a purely functional application as it applies to attention, concentration, mediation (or deep concentration) and even perhaps initiation. Just the sheer application of focused attention can achieve much and it is in this light that we can find this aspect of MENTALISM, by developing perception, understanding, and knowledge.

Also the process of initiation gives us the framework by which to understand a particular set of laws or principals within which to work, to create rather than merely to dream.

So too in the quote above, we are introduced to a familiar aspect of Freemasonry in the *"psychic temple of knowledge"* By extension we can equate this to the idea of King Solomon's temple as more than the idea of the wise kings allegorical building being constructed and perceive it as an opening to an intitiatic mechanism in which our knowledge, beliefs, spirit, and soul are linked together. This lesson seems an invaluable one as it establishes a connection to our external being and out internal wisdom. By developing that wisdom with the processes mentioned, we can truly find that Master-Key as referenced in the Kybalion.

This quest for the Master-Key is the inexorable process of the Masonic initiation and inculcation into Freemasonry's ancient fraternity. And it seems, in the nature of the Kybalion, that the quest for the Master-Key is the quest for this aspect of MENTALISM by an understanding of or own power of thought and concentration, which is the very spirit of the universe itself to which we are linked. This premise can be summarized as "I am, therefore, I create".

# THE PRINCIPLE OF CORRESPONDENCE

"As above, so below; as below, so above."
*-The Kybalion*

This Principle embodies the truth that **there is always a Correspondence between the laws and phenomena of the various planes of Being and Life.** The old Hermetic axiom ran in these words: *"As above, so below; as below, so above"* and the grasping of this Principle gives one the means of solving many a dark paradox, and hidden secret of Nature. *There are planes beyond our knowing, but when we apply the Principle of Correspondence to them we are able to understand much that would otherwise be unknowable to us.* This Principle is of universal application and manifestation, on the various planes of the material, mental, and spiritual universe— it is an **Universal Law.** The ancient Hermetists considered this Principle as one of **the most important mental instruments by which man was able to pry aside the obstacles which hid from view the Unknown.** Its use even tore aside the Veil of Isis to the extent that a glimpse of the face of the goddess might be caught. Just as a knowledge of the Principles of Geometry enables man to measure distant suns and their movements, while seated in his observatory, so **a knowledge of the Principle of Correspondence enables Man to reason intelligently from the Known to the Unknown.** Studying the monad, he understands the archangel.

*-The Kybalion*

This principal should come easily to most Freemasons, as it can quickly be related to the allegorical, or symbolic, correspondence to the degree system. When equated at an analogous level, we can see the planes of existence as levels of change and also as the degrees in Freemasonry. Upon our first approach to the lodge room door our perception of the fraternity is different than it will be in seconds, minutes, hours, days, months, years, and decades later. But even as it differs, it still resonates with our first principal perception in coming to that door.

Very early on we are taught the symbolism of the plumb, and the use of this tool to find our vertical path to the divine. It also illustrates our first place in the lodge as it is demarked by the point within the circle, which we come to know as our Center to the universe. This same illustration of elevation can appertain to our role in lodge as it progresses from us, to the lodge as a body, to the Grand Lodge, to which that body belongs, and to Freemasonry itself. Each step being characterized by our interaction with it.

This speaks to our symbolic understanding of one things relationship to another. We can see this, perhaps, in modern faith practice in the act of prayer which alludes to sending up our hopes and fears for divine intervention that we trust will intercede on our behalf. This is illustrative to past ages when the idea of GOD was perceived as a pantheon of man like deities who shared our own hopes, fears, and aspirations. This created in us an association of what transpires here in our mortal coil to what happens above in the celestial one, and conversely what happens above to us below. This is perceptible in our understanding of man created in GOD's image. Symbolically, if in this image we strive to attain that part which is divine, we are then, in effect, gods in GOD's image, but only as we see that force known as GOD as the divine artificer of creation rather than a manifestation of our baser tendencies. This exception is true as the divine can only be of a higher nature, and it is unique in each of our perceptions for how we conceive that force. Our existence is a mirror reflection of the existence beyond which could be interpreted as being one and the same.

Here too, in this short excerpt of the Kybalion we are reminded of Geometry and the lessons we take from its study. In the simple lesson of $a^2+b^2+c^2$ we can associate it to the perfection of its parts to solve the whole. This is not meant as a means to find the divine, but a way to symbolically see it in effect. To equate it on another level prayer with intent to manifest will produce the desired result. It is action that proceeds from thought.

From this principal we can see the correspondence of thought to action to result. Similarly it is the result of culmination by thought and action, our will becoming the manifestation of that divine influence manifesting through the results of our intent.

# THE PRINCIPLE OF VIBRATION

"Nothing rests; everything moves; everything vibrates."
*-The Kybalion.*

This Principle embodies the truth that "everything is in motion"; *"everything vibrates"*; *"nothing is at rest"*; facts which Modern Science endorses, and which each new scientific discovery tends to verify. And yet this Hermetic Principle was enunciated thousands of years ago, by the Masters of Ancient Egypt. *This Principle explains that the differences between different manifestations of Matter, Energy, Mind, and even Spirit, result largely from varying rates of Vibration.* From **THE ALL**, which is Pure Spirit, down to the grossest form of Matter, all is in vibration—the higher the vibration, the higher the position in the scale. The vibration of Spirit is at such an infinite rate of intensity and rapidity that it is practically at rest-just as a rapidly moving wheel seems to be motionless. And at the other end of the scale, there are gross forms of matter whose vibrations are so low as to seem at rest. Between these poles, there are millions upon millions of varying degrees of vibration. From corpuscle and electron, atom and molecule, to worlds and universes, everything is in vibratory motion. This is also true on the planes of energy and force (which are but varying degrees of vibration); and also on the mental planes (whose states depend upon vibrations); and even on to the spiritual planes. *An understanding of this Principle, with the appropriate formulas, enables Hermetic students to control their own mental vibrations as well as those of others.* The Masters also apply this Principle to the conquering of Natural phenomena, in various ways. "He who understands the Principle of Vibration, has grasped the sceptre of power," says one of the old writers.

*-The Kybalion*

This principal in some sense represents measurement and scale. Its early indication is that "all is in motion" and that "everything vibrates". These ideas seem obscure in the trade of free stone masons, but as with our past lessons, we need to take this principal in context. Here again we must perceive the degree as waves progressing out from a center point, even perhaps the point within a circle. These waves are a visual representation of our spiritual vibratory nature, and the emanations we create as we grow in the universe. Illustratively, we can see this in the motion of the compass as it renders the circumference of our circle in ever increasing & decreasing rings as we mature. As our interpretations grow, so to will they change, then by allowing us to re-circumscribe our understanding.

In this lesson too, we can find resonance with Pythagorean parable of tone and its relationship to other tones in a measurable progresses in scale[2]. As each note progresses in harmony, the motion and density of each notes wave expands or contracts to its corresponding tone.

Lastly, we can associate the working tools of all three degrees, as they are tools by which to measure the emanations of the vibrations that we encounter in everyday existence. Their use is not prescribed as such, but in their normal implementation they, by default, measure and grade the daily work that they produce. In this measure we are shaping, testing, and learning to control the very vibratory nature to which this principal alludes. All is a manifestation of vibration, even the exertion of our energy by thought and work to synthesize further thoughts and works.

Our title itself reflecting that scale as our spirit is free to work upon the immutable stone. Both are the extremes of the imperceptible vibration: one existing at so high a frequency that it is imperceptible to ordinary senses and measured only by the flowing circle made by an open compass. And the other so low a frequency as to share that same vibratory nature as the stone it was hewn from. This is the perfection and sublimity of the heavens and earth, the celestial and the firmament, the compass and the square. Between them exists the scale of our work as a Free Stone mason.

## THE PRINCIPLE OF POLARITY

"Everything is Dual; everything has poles; everything has its pair of opposites; like and unlike are the same; opposites are identical in nature, but different in degree; extremes meet; all truths are but half-truths; all paradoxes may be reconciled."
*-The Kybalion*

This Principle embodies the truth that *"everything is dual"*; *"everything has two poles"*; *"everything has its pair of opposites,"* all of which were old Hermetic axioms. It explains the old paradoxes, that have perplexed so many, which have been stated as follows: *"Thesis and antithesis are identical in nature, but different in degree"*; *"opposites are the same, differing only in degree"*; "the pairs of opposites may be reconciled"; "extremes meet"; "everything is and isn't, at the same time"; "all truths are but half truths"; "every truth is half-false"; "there are two sides to everything," etc., etc., etc. *It explains that in everything there are two poles, or opposite aspects, and that "opposites" are really only the two extremes of the same thing, with many varying degrees between them.* To illustrate: Heat and Cold, although "opposites," are really the same thing, the differences consisting merely of degrees of the same thing. Look at your thermometer and see if you can discover where "heat" terminates and "cold" begins! There is no such thing as "absolute heat" or "absolute cold"—the two terms "heat" and "cold" simply indicate varying degrees of the same thing, and that 'same thing" which manifests as "heat' and 'cold" is merely a form, variety, and rate of Vibration. So "heat" and "cold" are simply the "two poles' of that which we call "Heat"—and the phenomena attendant thereupon are manifestations of the Principle of Polarity. The same Principle manifests in the case of "Light and Darkness," which are the same thing, the difference consisting of varying degrees between the two poles of the phenomena. Where does "darkness" leave off, and "light" begin? What is the difference between "Large and Small"? Between "Hard and Soft"? Between "Black and White"? Between "Sharp and Dull"? Between "Noise and Quiet"? Between "High and Low"? Between "Positive and Negative"? *The Principle of Polarity explains these paradoxes, and no other Principle can supersede it. The same Principle operates on the Mental Plane.* Let us take a radical and extreme example-that of "Love and Hate," two mental states apparently totally different. And yet there are degrees of Hate and degrees of Love, and a middle point in which we use the terms "Like or Dislike," which shade into each other so gradually that sometimes we are at a loss to know whether we "like" or "dislike" or "neither." *And all are simply degrees of the same thing, as you will see if you will but think a moment.* And, more than this (and considered of more importance by the Hermetists), *it is possible to change the vibrations of Hate to the vibrations of Love, in one's own mind, and in the minds of others.* Many of you, who read these lines, have had personal experiences of the involuntary rapid transition from Love to Hate, and the reverse, in your own case and that of others. And you will therefore realize the possibility of *this being accomplished by the use of the Will*, by means of the Hermetic formulas. "Good and Evil" are but the poles of the same thing, and the Hermetist understands the art of transmuting Evil into Good, by means of an application of the Principle of Polarity. In short, the *"Art of Polarization becomes a phase of "Mental Alchemy" known and practiced by the ancient and modern Hermetic Masters. An understanding of the Principle will enable one to change his own Polarity, as well as that of others, if he will devote the time and study necessary to master the art.*

-*The Kybalion*

Freemasonry, at first blush, does not stand out as an organization that is illustrated with duality. It is only after entering the halls of its lodges do many of the subtle clues begin to appear. I mention duality as it is the distillation of the idea of polarity, as something opposite another. Specifically speaking to this aphorism of the Kybalion in Freemasonry we do find many instances of their existing examples in opposition. This is not necessarily to mean a positive and negative in the good/bad sense, but the existence of ideas that exist in the same context delineated by a line of thought or opinion. In their contrast by looking at them as dual ideas we can start to see and study this principal of polarity.

Our first indication of this is in our own becoming a Mason. In this act we immediately take the role of having not been one and then becoming one which places us centrally into this principal, the very symbols the fraternity itself illustrating this, in the pairing of the square and compass. But other symbols too strike this polarity upon our admission: the pillars, the Holy Saints John, and our passage from darkness into light. Each of these ideas strives to symbolize that even in unity we still exist within a dual nature.

Even as these seeming extremes exist on scale, they are measured in the distance between them. Here too we can find association with the 24 inch gage as their measure. It is with this scale that we can gage the manifestation of subduing out passion and depth of brotherly love. In doing this, we can control the polarity of these extremes and find their balance. In finding that equilibrium, we can apply the plumb to ascend to our ideal state.

An example of this balance of scale is aptly evident in the role and position of the candidate to the three principal stations of the lodge. As the neophyte enters into the lodge, they are said at various points to be in parallel with the three officers. The measures between them individually are exactly that position of duality. The candidate occupying the central position is identical in nature but different by degree. In this triangular construct, the Worshipful Master,

Senior and Junior Warden, and the candidate sum to the number of perfection in representing 10 degrees of scale. This is an emanation of the vibration measured in scale between them as each position has a point parallel to it. This is the manifestation of intent to action influenced only by where its position on scale resides. Interestingly, this configuration also signifies the perfection of the act itself placing the candidate at the center of the divine triangle and connecting him to 10 points, which also symbolize the divine perfection of the act.

Representatively, this is the essence of mental alchemy by the progressive transmutation from one state to another. Of not knowing to knowing - Of not being to becoming - To seek mastery and becoming a Master all representing the Masters Key to understanding this wisdom. It is in the scale that we can see the polarity of positions we occupy on this plane and in all we inhabit.

# THE PRINCIPLE OF RHYTHM

"Everything flows, out and in; everything has its tides;
all things rise and fall; the pendulum-swing manifests in
everything; the measure of the swing to the right is the
measure of the swing to the left; rhythm compensates."
-*The Kybalion*

This Principle embodies the truth that *in everything there is manifested a measured motion, to and fro; a flow and inflow; a swing backward and forward; a pendulum-like movement; a tide-like ebb and flow;* a high-tide and low-tide; *between the two poles which exist in accordance with the Principle of Polarity* described a moment ago. There is always an action and a reaction; an advance and a retreat; a rising and a sinking. *This is in the affairs of the Universe, suns, worlds, men, animals, mind, energy, and matter.* This law is manifest in the creation and destruction of worlds; in the rise and fall of nations; in the life of all things; and finally in the mental states of Man (and it is with this latter that the Hermetists find the understanding of the Principle most important). The Hermetists have grasped this Principle, finding its universal application, and have also discovered certain means to overcome its effects in themselves by the use of the appropriate formulas and methods. *They apply the Mental Law of Neutralization.* They cannot annul the Principle, or cause it to cease its operation, but they have learned how to escape its effects upon themselves to a certain degree depending upon the Mastery of the Principle. *They have learned how to USE it, instead of being USED BY it.* In this and similar methods, consist the Art of the Hermetists. *The Master of Hermetics polarizes himself at the point at which he desires to rest, and then neutralizes the Rhythmic swing of the pendulum which would tend to carry him to the other pole.* All individuals who have attained any degree of Self-Mastery do this to a certain degree, more or less unconsciously, but the Master does this consciously, *and by the use of his Will, and attains a degree of*

*Poise and Mental Firmness almost impossible of belief on the part of the masses who are swung backward and forward like a pendulum.* This Principle and that of Polarity have been closely studied by the Hermetists, and the methods of counteracting, neutralizing, and USING them form an important part of the Hermetic Mental Alchemy.

-The Kybalion

The logical step from the principal of polarity is aptly the principal of rhythm. In concluding polarity we left off with the transition of states: not knowing to knowing, seeking mastery to becoming a master, etc. Rhythm, as this principal alludes, is the energy exerted in such quests. But not as a base consumption of fuel to an exertion of force but the action involved in its exertion. This is similar to the idea of the journey between two places, the HOW something is achieved.

As we seek to understand Masonry, we are always in a state of motion, be it physical, mental emotional, spiritual or in being. This relates to our degrees as we transition from one state to another, collecting, growing, and discovering new insights to ourselves, the degrees, and how they relate to us.

So to, do we experience this in life. As we mature from birth, grow in manhood, and age in time. This is the rhythm of our existence picking up the things we discover anew, and throwing off the things we no longer find use for. This is a natural state of man, as our spirit is like stone; we chip and shape it daily.

Understanding this principal allows us to shape and hew ourselves and our perception to the world around us. And, in so doing, it helps us to grow and make future decisions. Science has taught us that very little is fixed in place, including the celestial heavens and firmament under our feet. And as such, neither is our perception or ideas so fixed. If properly applied we take from our Masonic degrees the knowledge to progress in this rhythm and dissuade regression transforming ourselves to the ideal state.

By seeing the process of rhythm, and controlling its motion, we can progress even further to so sublime a degree that we can master the vibration of our being and shape the vibration and rhythm of the world around us. This is the ultimate extension of our will, honed on the lessons of the Kybalion and shaped in the degrees of Freemasonry, manifested in our creation.

# THE PRINCIPLE OF CAUSE AND EFFECT

"Every Cause has its Effect; every Effect has its Cause;
everything happens according to Law; Chance is but
a name for Law not recognized; there are many planes
of causation, but nothing escapes the Law."
                                              -*The Kybalion*

This Principle embodies the fact that there is a Cause for every Effect; an Effect from every Cause. It explains that: *"Everything Happens according to Law"; that nothing ever "merely happens"; that there is no such thing as Chance; that while there are various planes of Cause and Effect, the higher dominating- the lower planes, still nothing ever entirely escapes the Law.* The Hermetists understand the art and methods of rising above the ordinary plane of Cause and Effect, to a certain degree, and *by mentally rising to a higher plane they become Causers instead of Effects. The masses of people are carried along, obedient to environment; the wills and desires of others stronger than themselves; heredity; suggestion; and other outward causes moving them about like pawns on the Chessboard of Life.* But the Masters, rising to the plane above, dominate their moods, characters, qualities, and powers, as well as the environment surrounding them, and become Movers instead of pawns. They help to PLAY THE GAME OF LIFE, instead of being played and moved about by other wills and environment. *They USE the Principle instead of being its tools. The Masters obey the Causation of the higher planes, but they help to RULE on their own plane.* In this statement there is condensed a wealth of Hermetic knowledge-let him read who can.

                                              -*The Kybalion*

Nothing occurs without a cause. All action is the rhythmic vibration reaction to another vibration and so on. The WILL, as a conscious manifestation, is merely the reaction of, or to, another manifestation of will. This is the root of cause and effect, which operates in us as humans and relates to the natural law.

In the degrees of masonry, we are introduced to the allegory of Hiram Abiff. In this allegory we symbolically are said to represent Hiram by taking his place to receive that lesson. We experience, first hand, the cause and effect of his destruction. But it is in this lesson that we assume both the role of the causation and effect of that intent. We are both ruffian and the victim.

In this allegory, however, we are taught the example by which to operate. We are instructed on the results of that cause and how to apply its law. Throughout we have had illustrated for us the Masonic principals by which to operate in teaching its ramification. The very use of the myriad tools of the degrees teaches us how to illuminate this principal. The cause and effect can be seen in each: the spreading of cement; the action of the plumb; the circumscription of the compass; and so on. Each of these functions has an implicit cause and effect that apply cumulatively to the whole. It is the causation of these actions that we can see, try, and implement their effectiveness in shaping their vibration.

Ultimately, we are not the causation of the degree, merely the student of it, and the passing of this knowledge becoming the source of our own the vibration - our spirit becoming the spirit of the fraternity.

This becomes the key to our Mastery.

# THE PRINCIPLE OF GENDER

"Gender is in everything; everything has its Masculine and
Feminine Principles; Gender manifests on all planes."
*-The Kybalion*

*This Principle embodies the truth that there is GENDER manifested
in everything—the Masculine and Feminine Principles ever at
work. This is true not only of the Physical Plane, but of the Mental
and even the Spiritual Planes.* On the Physical Plane, the Principle
manifests as SEX, on the higher planes it takes higher forms, but the
Principle is ever the same. *No creation, physical, mental or spiritual,
is possible without this Principle.* An understanding of its laws will
throw light on many a subject that has perplexed the minds of men.
The Principle of Gender works ever in the direction of *generation,
regeneration, and creation.* Everything, and every person, contains
the two Elements or Principles, or this great Principle, within it,
him or her. Every Male thing has the Female Element also; every
Female contains also the Male Principle. *If you would understand
the philosophy of Mental and Spiritual Creation, Generation, and
Re-generation, you must understand and study this Hermetic
Principle.* It contains the solution of many mysteries of Life. We
caution you that this Principle has no reference to the many base,
pernicious and degrading lustful theories, teachings and practices,
which are taught under fanciful titles, and which are a prostitution of
the great natural principle of Gender. Such base revivals of the ancient
infamous forms of Phallicism tend to ruin mind, body and soul, and
the Hermetic Philosophy has ever sounded the warning note against
these degraded teachings which tend toward lust, licentiousness, and
perversion of Nature's principles. If you seek such teachings, you
must go elsewhere for them—Hermeticism contains nothing for you
along these lines. *To the pure, all things are pure; to the base, all
things are base.*

*-The Kybalion*

To most Regular Masons, this principal may seem out of place, simply for the very reason that it speaks to the duality of men and women. But looking through the veil of Isis, we can find traits of the fraternity that speak to the union of masculine and feminine attributes, predominately in the very degrees themselves. By examination of the system, the sublime art is truly a manifestation of a creative force that links together the action and the will into a new creation, which is the very work of creating new Freemasons.

Symbolically, we can divide this into the labor of the lodge and the ritual that is performed which takes the form of masculine and feminine correspondence. A positive (+) and negative (-) aspect merge together and manifest through their union which results in the transformation of the initiate into the neophyte. This negative, however, is not an ill or corrupt force, but merely the opposition on scale to one another. Throughout the degrees, we find this principal in the sun and moon, the black and white pillars as illuminated on the tarot, and the level to the vertical plumb the square and compass. They are each in harmonious balance to one another to effect the candidate's creation.

In this principal we also receive a special caution which is the idea of not confusing the aspect of masculine and feminine with that of sexual gender or of propagation. Some who have confused this delineation have perverted it to become a symbol of a base generation. As tradition bears out, this Principal of Gender illuminates the separation of women and men in the aspect of this process. It is an act of theurgy, then, that is the union of these vibrations to become, by form and function, harmony together. That does not imply that it cannot be practiced outside of Freemasonry, but for this analysis it must be rendered in its specific way to achieve its ends.

We can associate the separation to the examples given us from alchemy in the process to achieve a high degree of purity in the minerals being transformed towards the creation of the Philosophers Stone. It is in this context that purity benefits the clarity of purpose to become the means of creation.

# FREEMASONRY AND THE KYBALION
## CONCLUSION

"As above, so below; as below, so above."
-*The Kybalion*

*MY THOUGHTS being once seriously busied about things that are, and my Understanding lifted up, all my bodily Senses being exceedingly holden back, as it is with them that are heavy of sleep, by reason either of fullness of meat, or of bodily labour: Me thought I saw one of an exceeding great stature, and of an infinite greatness, call me by my name, and say unto me, What wouldst thou hear and see? Or what wouldst thou understand to learn and know?*

*Then said I, Who are Thou? I am, quoth he, Poemander, the mind of the great Lord, the most mighty and absolute Emperor: I know what thou wouldst have, and I am always present with thee.*

*Then I said, I would learn the things that are, and understand the nature of them, and know God. How? said he. I answered that I would gladly hear. Then said he, Have me again in they mind, and whatsoever though wouldst learn, I will teach thee.*

*When he had thus said, he was changed in his Idea or Form, and straightway, in the twinkling of an eye, all things were opened unto me. And I saw an infinite sight, all things were become light, both sweet and exceeding pleasant; and I was wonderfully delighted in the beholding it.*

Corpus Hermetica - "Poemander."

The full text of the Kybalion is short and is the manifestation of the initiates of it in the early 20th Century, as indicated in the introduction. It is not a Rite, or degree system, but rather a transliteration of the Hermetic codex from 20 Centuries earlier, which are ideas from an even earlier period. Like any initiation, by reading them and attempting to understand them, you too become one of the initiates of its wisdom. Mastery, true Mastery, cannot be conferred by them but rather comes by true application and understanding of their meaning. It is not a state that ones arrives at instantaneously, but is shaped and formed over a lifetime, comparable to each of our perfect ashlars.

The seven Principals of the Kybalion are a philosophical set of ideas towards achieving the divine state, much like the degrees of Masonry which equates to our individual Mastery of them.

With the focus of Mentalism, we can envision the divine state to which we seek to achieve. In setting about this labor we find and seek Correspondence of one thing to another creating, through our thoughts their relationships from our plane to that of the divine, ultimately to our residence in that divine state. To achieve this we must first witness and take note of our governance of, and reaction to, the Vibratory emanations to which we are surrounded. "Everything vibrates" is the idea we are given and as such we are merely the source of and the recipients of such vibrations that exist. But of these vibrations, we must pay heed that they exist as Polarities to one another and can therefore be influenced by how we are influenced by them and so on. Our perception and will controlling how they resonate in finding their position, it is through their Rhythm that we begin to resonate with, or against, them and exude our influence. But in this influence we are grounded by their Effect and drive their Causation in how others interpret them. Lastly, we also find that there is another aspect that is a work which is the principal of Gender in which all vibrations resonate. Socially, we can see this as compromise and in creation as manifestation.

These ideas and aspects are not common to Freemasonry,

but are still vital in their intent by the teaching and promulgation of the fraternity's purpose. By understanding these principals, and the Kybalion, we can better attune their operation and function in our daily lives. By doing this, we can embark on a path to Mastery and unfold that inner lotus of knowing. By knowing, we take on the word of creation "I am" and become creators and shapers ourselves. It is here that we find the lost word in the lessons of the Kybalion which is the key to our Mastery as a Mason.

Hermes Trismegistus

# XIII
# So
# What?

The question above has been an institutional answer to a question that has plagued Masonry for the last 50 years, and when I first heard it's asking, I was not sure what to think about it. I wasn't even sure if I should talk about as it seems like an internal problem, and not the fodder for the rank and file to ponder. It wasn't until my own realization dawned that it was the rank and file that was ultimately the cause and effect of the question AND the answer, and that its implications became clear to me. And, as the adage goes, if you don't talk about it, how do you fix it? And with such a large fraternity I felt that we needed to talk about it.

In doing some research, I found myself at the web site for the MSANA, which is the *Masonic Service Association of North America*[1]. They are a National clearinghouse for all things Masonic, but specifically an informational collection agency that gathers data and publishes literature for the overall benefit of the craft.

One of the items I found there were statistics on membership from 1925 to 2005. The statistics are the national numbers of membership in the United States from 1930-2000. It was not graphed, so it was a pretty uninteresting grid of dates and numbers. From a surface analysis what it showed was an early high figure, a dip, a huge growth trend, and then a dramatic down trend in membership, specifically from a period of 1960 to today. The graph in *figure 1* was created from these statistics. What it charts is the membership numbers from 1925 to 2008.

For a comparison *figure 2* graphs the U.S. population in the same period. The numbers are dramatically different; Freemasonry at one to four million and the US population at 100 to almost 300 million, but what it illustrates by contrast is the dramatic rise in US population (about half of which are male +/- 51/49%) and the dramatic decrease to male membership. What I want to illustrate here is that as the US population has steadily increased, the population of Freemasonry has steadily decreased substantially.

So to the question, so what?

Most who have been members for a significant time know that the membership of Freemasonry is changing. Lodge rooms are seating fewer and fewer members, old buildings bought and built in the boom era are being sold off as membership roles shrink and charters evaporate, as if they never existed. We know that already, this isn't new information. Every Masonic publication has said this at some point or another that "our numbers are retracting, that we felt a boom with the returning vets of WWII and Korea, and that their numbers swelled our ranks to their record numbers, topping at a height of 4,103,161 in 1959". But since that high water mark we have been in a steady decline in membership.

Again the question, so what?

The decline of the 1960's and 70's is often blamed on the

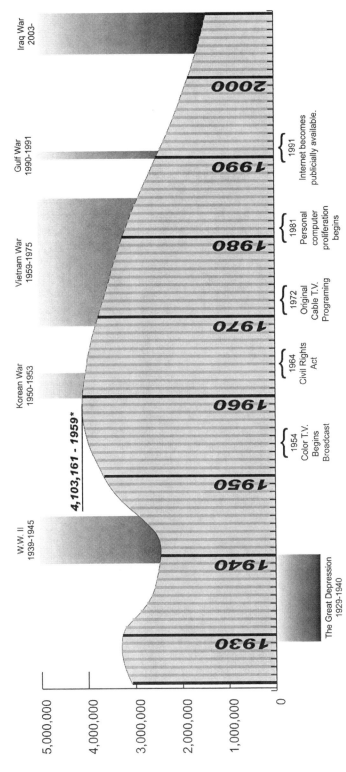

Figure 1.

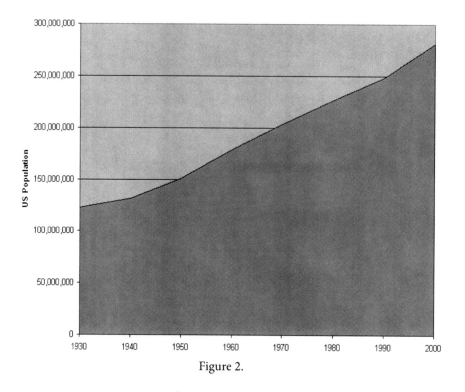

Figure 2.

selfish attitudes of the "tuned out" generation, the hippy turned Baby-Boomer, with widespread distrust of past paternal institutions, and a growth in a personal individuality, no one wanted to join, even when they later came of age the attitude of *"Forget doing what Dad did"* and *"why do I want to be a part of a secret institution of good old boys"* prevailed. But was that really the problem?

I'm sure if analyzed completely, academically, we could explore the *"why Freemasonry changed"* notion in the 60's, 70's, and 80's, but that is not the intent of this exploration. Some have suggested it was the institutional change towards fraternalism. Others suggest that it picked up and patriotic flavor of Americanism with the high number of veterans that came to its ranks. Trying to associate the increase to any one reason is difficult at best. What the numbers do tell us is that in 10 year intervals, from 1960 to 2005, membership dropped by an average of 560,152 members. On the graph, you can see the decline to 2005. Distilling the numbers, it comes out to an average of a 20% decrease in membership per 10-year period.

By the years it breaks out to:

1959, membership at its height was at 4,103,161

1960 - 1970 there was a loss of 336,006 a decrease of 8.19%

1970 - 1980 there was a loss of 511,685 a decrease of 13.597%

1980 - 1990 there was a loss of 719,885 a decrease of 22.14%

1990 - 2000 there was a loss of 690,474 a decrease of 27.274%

2000 - 2010* there was a loss of 542,714 a decrease of 29.477%

(*Calculated by doubling the loss from 2000 to 2005)

The average loss was 20% (20.2%)

Again the question "so what", we already know this, these numbers are not secret. They are published in an open forum for the public to see.

The overall calculation led to an extrapolation, if the fraternity lost on average 560,152 members, per year for the next 10-year cycle, from 2010 to 2020, our national number of members would be under 1 million members at 738,303. In ten more years 2020 to 2030 our national member base would be 178,151.

That number again is **One hundred and seventy eight thousand, one hundred and fifty one** TOTAL Freemason's in North America by 2030, which led me to speculate that the last American Freemason would probably be somewhere in about 2034 or so.

OK, so this is a worst-case scenario, this is an assumption that we will continue to lose the same 560,000 members a year, due to attrition, brothers passing, or low community interest. The overall numbers tell me that the loss % per year is INCREASING; not decreasing, but maybe the trend is just that, a trend. It should be said that at present, 2005 numbers show our fraternity at numbers lower than the 1925 watermark, when the US population was less than half of what it is today. What it appears is that what is happening is not just a "correction", that it is not simply the Fraternity going back to the "way things were" at the turn of the 20th century. That it is something much worse at play and further outside the scope of our control.

But, taken from another angle, we can say that over the same 50-year period, we did average out to a 20% loss per year. These numbers are far less frightening and show a slower descent over the next one hundred years. In 2030, where the first model takes us to extinction in the percentage model we sit at just over 800,000 members. It isn't until 2130 that we get to fewer than 100,000. But again, that is at a steady 20% decrease no ups, no downs, steady. The trend on the last 50-year cycle has been one of a steady increase in percentage loss, 8.9%, 13.59%, 22.14%, 27.27%, and 29.47%. This model, though more positive, seems less likely.

At the other end of the spectrum, some locations so seem to indicate an upward trend in membership. In areas that lost 4000 members, they took in 2000, diminishing the overall drop, but even these anecdotal statistics only suggest a change in trend without much ability to forecast realistically where the descent will level off. Again the question, so what?

With those of us left, we become the inheritors of Freemasonry here in America, and need to address the question of what we are going to do about it. I have read a *Laudable Pursuit*[2], as I am sure many other masons have, I attend meetings, pay my dues, and heed the length of my cable tow but is that enough? Are dynamic meetings, meaningful Masonic education, Traditional Observance Lodges, Festive Boards, or low cost spaghetti or fish fry dinners the answer? Even the boldest Grand Lodge programs, like the Massachusetts Ben

Franklin Marketing Campaign or the California Masonic Formation movement, enough? What generated interest in the past?

To answer this we need to ask what Freemasonry has lost. What component of our fraternity did we lose in the transition of the 1950's into the 1990's that closed us off from the moral imagination of society? What changed? Was it the success of the offshoot "clubs" whose focus on charity or drama plays rather than esoteric meaning took prominence? Did we, institutionally, become afraid of what our own metaphysical/spiritual fraternity represented? Were we marginalized as an increasing religious America took dominance over a more embracing ecumenical institution towards all faith traditions? Did American Freemasonry fall out of progressive step with the evolving landscape of American women's issues, and racial equality taking the forefront but still at odds in the fraternity dedicated to the moral high ground? It was in the periods of transition from the 19th to the 20th century that many esoteric or occult works were created that seem to evoke the spirit of the coming age of Masonry.[3] Did their promise grow silent on the lips of those who took the reins of leadership? Just one small marker I can point to, that symbolically illustrates the transition was the name change of the monthly Scottish Rite magazine from the then *New Age Magazine* to the now *Scottish Rite Journal* in 1989. Its true that in the mid century a degree of quackery took hold of the metaphysical, from the psychic to tarot parlor readers, but did our hasty retreat from all things esoteric help steer the fraternity towards the rocks of obscurity? Did we become afraid of our own esoteric aegis marginalizing our own traditions and effectively doing this to ourselves? The one thing that so many outsiders look to Freemasonry to provide, a degree of esoteric wisdom and education we can barely articulate to the simple question of *"what does Freemasonry represent?"* Its tradition pointing one way with progressive learning and metaphysical death/rebirth; its members pointing another with fraternalism, patriotism, and civic engagement, is it a social club or a path to self enlightenment?

As the numbers continue to descend, some possible scenarios to consider is the separation of the Shrine from the craft lodge system. With the success that the Shrine has enjoyed in this last century, why would they keep the requirement of the Blue Lodge membership, if the blue lodge can barely support itself let alone its wealth of sponsored charity. Especially in the face of diminished revenue and potential loss of its charitable hospital arm. In its present configuration, can it afford to not take in now blue lodge members?

Another such scenario is the separation of the Scottish Rite, as a degree raising body. What is to keep them from offering the degrees as more Craft lodges start to close? The easy answer is, of course not, but as membership continues to plummet, at what point will desperation take hold and other options become more enticing? Is the American Rites prepared to close operations if memberships diminish to an unsustainable level?

So what, what can we do about this?

The most effectual answer I can come up with, individually, to the "SO WHAT" question is nothing. We can, at this point in time do nothing to turn this trend around. No matter how many open houses, public lectures, marketing campaigns, sports sponsorships, television commercials, radio spots, billboards, or finite programs promoted by Grand Lodges will stem this hemorrhage. Even if we started giving away memberships, it's doubtful that we could find enough people who even remembered who the Freemasons are, and even fewer who would want to become one.

The damage is already done, and we are now in for a further declination that will erase what is left of North American Freemasonry. This means the closure and roll back of individual state Grand Lodges. This will mean the selling of more Masonic assets, and the selling or divesting publicly of our privately funded billion dollar institutions.

This means the end of Freemasonry, as we know it today.

But this does not mean that all is lost and that there are things that we can do now to start to effect change. The greatest change will come in our perception of what the fraternity represents and that its history, both real and imagined, is a part of who we are. And by understanding that, we can embrace it and celebrate that diversity and begin to explore anew those ideas from a century ago. Also, as a body, we can pause and consider out institution and how it relates to the broader civil society. Is our venerable institution living up to the premise that our very Rites espouse? Do we treat ALL people equally, no matter of Race, gender, or preference? Are we striving to make social progress?

In the next 30 years the landscape of what we call "Regular Freemasonry" will be radically different than what we see today. The sooner we come to recognize that, talk about it, and confront it head on the sooner we can start planning on what we want to do about it. Burying our heads in the sand is not the answer. If we continue to insist on doing this, it will only further hasten our demise. Our generation is the unwilling inheritor of the future of Freemasonry. What we do now dictates how our sons will come to know this ancient institution. If we ignore this problem, there won't be any institution left.

If you don't take my word for it, look at the numbers for your self and draw your own conclusions. Once you've drawn them, however, I challenge you to act on them.

# XIV
# King Solomon's Temple

*A Symbol to Freemasonry*

Solomon's ancient temple was built a top Mt. Moriah in Jerusalem between 964 and 956 B.C.E. It's construction is chronicled in the First Book of Kings, which begins at the end of King David's reign and the crowning of Solomon. As king, Solomon continues the task his father began which was to build the temple. The text tells us that God restricted David, having collected the materials to construct the temple, from building it because of the blood he shed at the conquering of Israel. Ultimately, Solomon completes work on the temple, which was built to house the Ark of the Covenant, and become *"a glorious temple for which God was to dwell"*. (1 Kings 8:13).

Chris Hodapp, in his manual *"Freemasons for Dummies"*, defines Solomon's Temple as a representation of the individual Freemason, where both an individual man and the physical temple take "many years to build" as a *"place suitable for the spirit of God to inhabit"*.[1] The work of a becoming a Freemason is, in my opinion, a metaphor to the construction of the temple. This definition is not far off the mark, but alone it says nothing of why this bold metaphor is used.

Through deeper explorations of this topic, I was lead to a broader understanding of the temple and its relevance to the Freemasonry we practice today. One path of that exploration led me to understand it from the perspective explored in the works of John Dee, Henry Cornelius Agrippa and Francesco Giorgi, each an important Renaissance philosopher.

In Dame Frances Yates text *The Occult Philosophy in the Elizabethan Age*, she suggests that early Renaissance Cabalists felt the temple represented a definition of sacred geometry that was mirrored in the temple by reflecting a perfect and proportional measure made *"in accordance with the unalterable laws of cosmic geometry."*[2] These ideas formed from the work of Francesco Giorgi in *De Harmonia Mundi*, which drew in Vitruvian principals of Architecture and integrated the foundation of Christian Cabalism with the ideas from Hermetic study to create "connections between angelic hierarchies and planetary spheres" that [rose] "up happily through the stars to the angels hearing all the way those harmonies on each level of the creation imparted by the Creator to his universe, founded on number and numerical laws of proportion".

These ideas are from an early Christian Cabala (c.1525), before the open appearance of Freemasonry, and Solomon's temple, as we know it today. Building on the ides of Giorgi, Cornelius Agrippa explored the ideas of Alchemy, Hermetic, Neoplatonic and Cabalist thought, and wrote about them in his book *De Occulta Philosophia*, published in 1533. In this text, one important idea was that the universe was divided into three worlds (degrees), which consisted of an elemental world, a celestial world, and an intellectual world, each receiving influences from the one above it. The first world was believed governed by natural magic (element) and arranged substances "in accordance with the occult sympathies between them". The second world is concerned with celestial magic that governed "how to attract and use the influences of the stars". Agrippa himself calling it "a kind of magic mathematical magic because its operations depend on number". The third world represented ceremonial magic "as directed toward the super celestial world of angelic spirits". Beyond that, Agrippa says, is the divine itself. These ideas are not about the physical temple, but instead I see it representing an unseen or perhaps inner temple, the travel in what we call today the self.[3]

This philosophy of this divine self, interacting with the magical principals I suggest, merged at that time into the then strong and intelligent stone mason guilds, blending their practical application of numbers and formulation with the exploration of the divine worlds that many worked to physically construct. These ideas were accepted and adopted into the early landmarks of Freemasonry where, I believe, the temple was perceived as more than a representational place of being. Over time, as philosophy and understanding changed, much of the fraternity lost sight of why Solomon's Temple was important, that it represented a more mystical and philosophical construct akin to Agrippa's spheres. Its interpretation has, today, moved into a metaphorical position becoming a part of the metaphorical stage in which our craft is set. But by examining how the temple exists in our degrees today will see some of that connection to the Renaissance philosophy.

Today, King Solomon's Temple, in Freemasonry appears in each of the three degrees (or worlds) as different aspects unique to that degree. Within the first, it is represented as the ground floor, the allegorical entrance into the fraternity. The temple is not depicted as the complicated structure; instead it is as an unfinished edifice, which is implicit to the ritual. Like Agrippa's first elemental sphere, the first degree of masonry is the initiate's entry point into Freemasonry and its philosophy, giving the initiate the elemental components to start his formation, only the work is not the rough labor of the operative, but instead the work of the speculative.

The second Degree makes use of the temples middle chamber, whose dual meaning represents the halfway point into the temple, and the halfway point of Freemasonry. But interestingly we are taught here that the second degree is the most important of the three degree, as it is here we are lead through the 15 steps from the ground floor to the middle chamber of King Solomon's Temple, where we as masons are instructed on our "wages due and jewels". The various adornments of the temple have a multifaceted meaning that is described in this degree, which again factor into the representation of the temple.

But what makes this degree so important is that it is not the middle chamber, but the odyssey across the three, five and seven steps to reach its summit. Across those steps we are taught about the three stages of human life, the five orders of architecture, and the seven liberal arts (amongst other things), and like Agrippa's second sphere of celestial magic, its mathematical influence can be felt throughout.[4]

This path is the important symbolic link to the temple, where our ritual goes so far to remind us that of the three degrees, the Fellowcraft is the one that applies *"our knowledge to the discharge of our respective duties to God, our neighbor, and ourselves; so that when in old age, as Master Masons, we may enjoy the happy reflections consequent on a well spent life, and die in the hopes of a glorious immortality."*[5] The emphasis being placed the lesson learned and the results of such diligent work.

The third degree, or the consequence of that well spent life, ultimately represents the Sanctum Sanctorum or Holy of Holies in King Solomon's Temple. Mentioned at the end of the Fellowcraft, this is where the brother reflects on the "well spent life" by the rewards of his work. The symbolism here is that it is the deepest heart of the temple and the furthest attainment of a Freemason. It also is to represent the deepest penetration into the psyche of the man. This is also the pinnacle of the ritual without the further exploration of the additional rites. The Holy of the Holies is representational of the celestial realm defined by Agrippa, and is the closest sphere outside of the divine itself. It functions as the house of God, both literally in the constructed temple, and metaphorically within the newly raised Mason. This echoes the ideas mentioned by Giorgi and later expanded on by Agrippa and Dee. Dee's further expansive ideas later went on to influence early Rosicrucian thought in a similar fashion.

Agrippa's three worlds, I suggest, form (in part) the basis of the steps and the journey through King Solomon's Temple through the degrees of Freemasonry. The presence of King Solomon's Temple in ancient thought, from the earliest Old Testament writings to the pinnacle of renaissance occult philosophy has preserved it as an iconographic representation of the path to the divine. Solomon's temple is not a solitary place in history, used as a simple metaphor in which to base an allegorical play. Instead, it is a link in early Christian Cabala and Hermetic thought, which is just as vital today, as it was then, to the tradition of Freemasonry, to define and create a construct to relate our movement through its several chambers. Just as it represented the pinnacle of holy practice, so to can it be equated to our own spiritual development by progressive degrees. It is still a metaphor worth of deeper reflection and thought. Looking at the ideas of this renaissance occult philosophy, I believe that these ideas become squarely linked to the past, present, and future of Freemasonry and to King Solomon's Temple.

# XV
# SAINT JOHN THE BAPTIST DAY

*My thanks to Ken Kolchier for his guided wisdom*
*in constructing this thesis.*

The Saints Johns appear to Freemasons in several places in our catechisms. Their proximity and use in our rituals have been questioned for many years as to their use and placement. Looked at together, saint John the Baptist and St. John the Evangelist serve to represent the balance in Masonry between zeal for the fraternity and learned equilibrium. The Saints John, stand in perfect parallel harmony representing that balance.

From a historical approach, The Saint John's festival is said to be a widely celebrated Masonic holiday. Traditionally June 24th (or the summer Solstice) is taken to be John the Baptist's day, which is celebrated in many cultures around the world. According to McCoy's Masonic Dictionary, the Festival of St. John in summer is a duty of every Mason to participate in, and should serve to be a renewal and strengthening of fraternal ties and a celebration of Masonry from "olden times". It functions as a connection between the past and the future.

The festival, to non-Masons, has been called the "Setting of the Watch", where ceremonial bonfires were lit after sunset. Tradition says that men, women, and children would jump through the fires for luck. Across Europe, this holiday is celebrated in many ways. With oak wreath crowns, wild flowers and birch branches. Families would feast and celebrate in union. The meanings of these ancient traditions are lost today on our modern society, but the link was made at some point to John the Baptist. The On-line Catholic Encyclopedia[1] points to the birth of John the Baptist as 6 months before Christ, placing him on the summer solstice. It is thought that these festivals have been linked in character and content with the birth of John the Baptist.

From the Masonic perspective we are given the balanced dualism of John the Baptist on one side and John the Evangelist on the other. Represented together this way represent the balance of passionate zeal with and learned knowledge of faith forming a space to reflect on to and channel our passion as well as our education/ knowledge. Individually strong, together they stand as a harnessed focus of zeal and knowledge. This counterpoint is not just necessary

to Freemasonry but can be applied to all areas of life. Taken as an abstract compilation of symbols, together they represent a well-balanced path towards enlightenment.

The two dualistic figures as one, the Holy Saints John, balance each other in the Masonic year, but also in other areas too. One unique aspect that I found is in the application of the Alchemical symbols of fire and water. Alchemy has long been thought of as an early component of Freemasonry and using the alchemical symbols here may help the representations of the Saint John's look more familiar. Saint John the Baptist, represented as the inverted pyramid, the Alchemical sign for water, representing the spiritual and emotional love. St. John the Evangelist, represented as the pyramid pointing up symbolizing fire that is the drive and will of action. When placed together, they symbolize the perfect balance of darkness and light, life and death, passion and constraint, will and emotion, winter and summer. Together both represent the interlocked star of Solomon, or the Square and Compass. This is an entirely open analysis, and made for the purposes of comparison, but it does offer a unique analysis of the juxtaposition of the Holy Saints John.

In looking toward the future, St. John the Baptist Day is an appropriate day for Freemasons, as it is a good day to come together and reflect in out past and in our future. It stands to remind us, not just of our past, but also of a recommitment of our circumscribed passions. In all of our time they're as a fraternity, union celebrations such as this one help us to reaffirm our ties that bind. Whether those ties be the bindings of fraternity or the familiarity of institution, we should remember the Holy Saints John's, not just in our sacred Jerusalem's but together in brotherhood.

# XVI
# SAINT JOHN THE EVANGELIST

December 27th is Saint John the Evangelist day, which is the 2nd feast day in the year to celebrate the Holy Saints John. The placement of the holiday also marks the winter solstice, which is directly opposite Saint John the Baptist's day at the summer solstice in June making a notable completion in the cycle of the solar year. The actual dates coincide with the solar calendar, creating the link is in the symbolism between them.

But why John the Evangelist, and what about him represents the counter balance of John the Baptist, the opposite pillar of the point within the circle? For those who forget, the point within the circle is the Masonic symbol that all men are said to endeavor to emulate in their physical and spiritual being. It essentially is the balancing ones desires and passions in the pursuit of knowledge.

As mentioned for John the Baptist, the two paired saints representing zeal and equilibrium on the sides of the circle.

Saint John the Baptist, represented as the inverted pyramid, the

Alchemical sign for water, representing the spiritual and emotional love. St. John the Evangelist, represented as the pyramid pointing up symbolizing fire that is the drive and will of action. When placed together, they symbolize the perfect balance of darkness and light, life and death, passion and constraint, will and emotion, winter and summer. Together both represent the interlocked star of Solomon, or the Square and Compass.

So who was John the Evangelist? Known for several things he is most notable as the only disciple of Christ to not forsake Him in the hour of His Passion at the foot of the cross, and he was the first to reach the tomb. When he met the risen Lord at the lake of Tiberius he was the first to recognize Him. Also, he is also attributed as the writer of the Epistles of John, and the book of Revelation. His feast day is said to have first been mentioned in the Sacrament of Pope Adrian I near 772 A.D.[1]

The Evangelist is also called the Apostle of Charity, which may be in part, his connection to Freemasonry. Or perhaps it is his unwavering resolve and purity for his love of the divine. The message to take from John the Evangelist is to "Apply thyself", therefore, to purity of heart, and thou shalt be like Saint John, a beloved disciple of Jesus, and shalt be filled with heavenly wisdom".

The feast is little remembered today, except in passing by a few lodges that gather together to celebrate it. It was once a high feast day for Freemasonry because of its proximity to the holidays and the presence of lodge members being close to home. It gave them a festival to meet under to punctuate the closing of the year. Meeting like this though is something not so convenient in this modern day as everyone travels abroad for the holiday. The shift in social communion however should not be so diminished and should play a larger role in the life of a lodge.

In the days following Christmas, pause for a moment to reflect on remember the feast day of Saint John the Evangelist, that pillar on the opposite side of John the Baptist balancing that circumscribed point within a circle and reflect on your brothers both present and absent, and reconnect with the fraternity you are a part of.

*1° Masonic Tracing Board*
*Digital Media*
*Greg Stewart, 2006*

# XVII
# 1° MASONIC TRACING BOARD

*A Symbolic Description*

Freemasonry is a tradition of initiation comprised of many elements from varying historical sources. As an initiatic tradition, its ceremonies consist of elaborate and dramatic rituals little changed in the hundreds of years of their existence. These ceremonies are a means to convey visual and descriptive allegories and metaphors to impart aspects of knowledge held valuable to the tradition that they serve to describe. The degrees of freemasonry, together, communicate the sum of these values; where the act of this initiation represents a movement, from an external space, to an internal one. This movement, as represented in the physical universe, is both a physical projection countered by an internal spiritual realization. Together, the external and internal journey of the man is represented here in this illustration of the First Degree Masonic Tracing Board. The vision of this board is a means to facilitate the personal movement into the sacred holy space. That sacred space is represented by the lodge itself and is entered into by ones movement in the degree and at the same time, an internal movement, traveled to by the meaning of the words and ceremony of the initiation. The rite itself becoming a metaphorical process of alchemical transformation for the candidates raw uninitiated spirit. What the initiation seeks to transform is the initiate's perception of themselves, their world, the dimensions above and beyond them and how they relate to each of them. The purposes of the degrees of Freemasonry are to make the candidate aware of their own ability and encourage them to seek the manner in which to make use of them, ultimately connecting them with their own inner divinity. This idea of transformation follows a line back to a time before the modern birth of Freemasonry in 1717[1], from ideas nurtured in the renaissance after being rediscovered by pre-renaissance aristocracy.[2] What had been saved were texts that had existed from a time before the fall of the Roman Empire. These works originated from manuscripts that at one time lived in the library of Alexandria[3] from traditions bourn out of the flood-waters and sand of Egypt. This does not mean that the tradition is the same as what these ancient peoples practiced, but rather what was passed forward is a tradition of Hermetic[4] philosophy, whose quest for the individual mystical transformation is itself the link to Freemasonry. In its most ancient and primordial state, Freemasonry emerges out of this ancient philosophy associated with the deity Thoth, the communicator of the Egyptian Gods, who the Greeks called Hermes Trismegistus, and the later Romans, Mercury. This tradition of Egyptian "occult knowledge"[5] was communicated to those neophytes capable, able, and willing to understand, and followed the model of the messenger to the gods Thoth, whose divinity was loosely associated as the communicator (messenger) between them. Similarly, that connection to communication has made its way into the tradition of Freemasonry by making and communicating its message, in both its ritual and symbols, including tracing boards like this one.

Like most systems, before you can comprehend its ultimate message it is necessary to examine it from the beginning, and in Freemasonry our beginning is at the initiation of the first degree, aptly called the "Entered Apprentice". The answer to these initial questions of "Who are you?" "What is it?" and "Why...?" start to take shape as the initiate, who has chosen to seek the answers, make the necessary travels to find them. This journey brings them to the threshold of the fraternity, better known in Freemasonry as the metaphorical entry porch of King Solomon's temple.

Modern Freemasonry begins this process by placing the initiate at the porch of the temple of Solomon, the holiest of holy shrines, built by the wisest of all kings. The original temple was, as chronicled in I Kings[6], built to house the second copy of the Ten Commandments.[7] This historic abode was considered by several faiths to be the holiest domicile known to man, becoming literally the "House of God". Symbolically, it took on the property of becoming God's celestial lodging here on earth. David, the conqueror of Israel, was charged with preparing the temple construction, but it was his son, Solomon, who was commanded to build it. It is Solomon's temple that Freemasonry has chosen to adopt into their allegories as the temple all Freemasons are said to enter into. This symbol likely entered into the allegory at a point when the traditions of European stone masons merged with esoteric alchemists[8] who found a commonality between the personal occult transformation that Hermetica taught and the external construction of the house of God. In time the two ideas came together, and the house of God was brought into the allegorical symbols and made an integral component of the initiation practice.

The tracing boards, simply described, are a collection of allegorical symbols uniquely arranged in a peculiar fashion to illustrate the degree to which they are associated. Pictographically, the illustration of the first degree represented on this tracing board, is the symbolic path of the initiate as he enters into the space of the Temple of Solomon. As such, entry is only granted to the pure of motivation and spirit for the purpose of education and enlightenment by means of certain symbolic devices made use of to instruct. One of the most profound lessons taught in this degree is duality, taught by the building of ideas and meaning. This duality however is often represented by triple meanings, as one thing is juxtaposed with another, and then yet another. In some instances, all three when taken together can meaning something else entirely. But these ideas will make themselves clearer as we explore specific aspects of the board.

As mentioned previously the tracing board is both a representation of Solomon's temple and the inner personal temple through the entry of the self[9]. Starting from an external position, the candidate approaches the board in the same manner as he approaches the degree, from a position without moving into a position within. The act is represented by the thought to ask the question and then acting upon its answer. The candidate accepts the offer to become a Mason, after petitioning, making the conscious decision to undergo the initiation. This decision sets him onto a path into the unknown. By making that decision, it starts his progress moving into the sacred space over a broad black and white checkerboard pavement. The checkered tile is representative of the sacred space that all masons are said to work upon. The mosaic is an expressive form of light and dark, good and evil, and a first physical example of the duality this degree suggests. It takes on the attribute of the space all of us are said to occupy and exist within. The tessellated, or triangular, borders mark the entry point into this plane that crossing over serves as a clear indication of our shift from the mundane world of man to that of the sacred. Within this space the initiate encounters three pillars that represent much in this allegory.

Derived from the text of Vitruvius[10], the pillars are of the Doric, Ionic, and Corinthian orders of architecture. In the lodge, and upon the tracing board, the pillars are meant to interpret as both literal and figurative in their representation of support.

Individually, the pillars with their ancient forms represent specific ideas that compose the lodge. And it is in those forms that we can equate certain aspects of the lodge by which we can describe the various parts of the temple. Those forms are:

**Doric**
*Wisdom*
*To Contrive the Temple*

**Ionic**
*Strength*
*To Support the Temple*

**Corinthian**
*Beauty*
*To Adorn the Temple*

These three pillars also correlate to the three principal leadership positions of the lodge as the W. Master, the Senior, and Junior Warden. Additionally, Masonic ritual[11] says that the pillars are parallel to the three great lights of masonry, which are said to be the sun, moon and master. The names correlate to the position of the pillars in the lodge. These positions represent a patriarchy in the lodge of three wise men and further represent a "spiritual synthesis" of perfection creating a stabilizing triangle with its three points, the balance to the struggle within the dual being. In essence, they represent the three points of a triangle, analogous to the sun, moon, and earth, which rule and guide the candidate on his Earthly journey.

These three constructs, however, give us a focus of the three parts, pointing inward guiding the candidate in his entry to the lodge. That central point of the candidate taking the middle position is the focus of the initiation, and the receiver of the instruction from the three wise magi. That instruction guides the candidate onto the sacred space, upon which he is confronted with a decision: to continue on or turn back. Being within the space, he has made is his decision

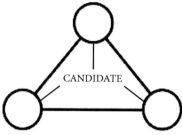

CANDIDATE

to continue, passing through on this spiritual quest when he is confronted by a perplexing symbol of ascent.

There before him, in this space is a simple ladder, allegorically referred to as Jacob's ladder, which represents the gateway between the earthly world and that of the divine. In the Bible, Jacob's ladder was the spiritual highway, which Jacob witnessed angels ascending and descending, between this world and the next. The vision coming to Jacob him in a dream, as told in Genesis 28:10, which says:

*"Jacob left Beersheba and set out for Haran. When he reached a certain place, he stopped for the night because the sun had set. Taking one of the stones there, he put it under his head and lay down to sleep. He had a dream in which he saw a stairway resting on the earth, with its top reaching to heaven, and the angels of God were ascending and descending on it...."*

The ladder represents the ascent that the initiate undertakes towards discovering the divine, but before the initiate can make his ascent he must first encounter three muses/virtues, known as Faith, Hope, and Charity. In some instances, the muses are depicted graphically to which they are shown as the anchor of faith, the holy sign of hope, and the heart of charity. Together, they keep trinity with the theme of three meanings in one. Individually, they symbolize three very important principals any aspirant should hold inviolate which are a faith in the divine (God), an unshaken and resolved anchor like hope of immortality, and a depth of compassion (charity) and love towards all mankind. Additionally, these three act as gatekeepers and are to gird the fortitude of the initiate and ensure he is worthy and qualified to make the ascension of the ladder. The journey up the ladder is not addressed, as it is the act of the degree itself that is considered the ascent. By undertaking the trial of the degree, the ladder becomes the passage to the next lesson, reached in the second degree.

As the ladder is central to the degree, there are other symbols of equal importance. Amongst the broader sets of images are categories with a more literal and direct meaning. These symbols are often referred to as jewels, and are divided into two sub sets of three, often referred to as "immovable", the other "moveable". The first set of three are the square, level and plumb which correspond to the three pillars and represent three cardinal compass points and their moral equivalents which are represented in this diagram below.

**Doric**
*Wisdom = Junior Warden*
*plumb = south = rectitude of life.*

**Ionic**
*Strength = Senior Warden*
*Level = West = Equality.*

**Corinthian**
*Beauty = Worshipful Master*
*Square = East = Morality.*

North has been omitted as symbolically in King Solomon's Temple, the north side of the temple was above the ecliptic and in shadow throughout the year. Masonic tradition considers the north as a place of darkness.

These tools are said to be immovable because of their permanence in the lodge, and in life. Additionally they are referred to as jewels for the beauty they strive to help find in a well earned life. The square defined both as a 90-degree angle on its corner, and a true perpendicular right angle as it relates our life to our spiritual (vertical) ascent, existing as a right angle projecting upwards. This is a bisection of morality as it relates to the divine.

It is important to note that it is not parallel with, nor tangential to, but a direct angle to the level. Its purpose is a direct relationship to our life and to the divine above. The level  is said to be the symbol of equality where all men exist, especially masons. This plane is one side of the square upon which we exist, awaiting a perfect conjunction with the divine. This is emblematic of our progression from the west towards the realm of the divine in the east, which is in conjunction of the level with the perpendicular This interpretation is made with the Plumb, as it is the measure of rectitude of life and a tool that is used to measure each individuals own existence from what ever their vantage. It is with this tool that a Mason can find his path upwards as he progresses upon his level of existence no matter its inclination in life. The plumb forever reminds the individual of Jacob's upright ladder that we forever seeks to attain. The purpose of these three items, as with their cardinal compass points, and officer positions within a lodge, are fixed and immutable, meaning they do not outwardly change. The holders of these offices and the individuals applying the principals may change, but not the devices themselves. Each of us is charged to measure our own existence and maintain them with these allegorical tools. These tools also serve as one of the first examples in the degrees by which masonry links itself to a lineage of temple builders as they are physical implements of construction.

Unlike the immovable jewels, the moveable jewels are elements of transition (movement); each with its own characteristic of change, and in their totality represents a state of progressive development. The moveable jewels are the rough ashlar (or un-worked stone), the perfect ashlar (hewn stone), and the trestle board (drawing board). These three items are independent of one another, but at the same time each item is an element in the same process, the planned transformation from a rough and imperfect state to a well developed true cube. Never do they wholly exist together, but never are they separate from each other either. These three items, like the alchemy they have come to represent, symbolize the state of change inherent in the system of Freemasonry. Individually, the rough ashlar represents the new initiate in his unrefined state.

Described by Pike as an untamed force, the rough ashlars represent the raw and unformed candidate, whose entry into Freemasonry begins to shape to his refinement. The perfect ashlar is symbolic to the initiate's transformation, the end result of his elevation through the degrees toward his attainment of the degree of Master Mason. Lastly the trestle board, or drawing table, is the plane upon which the transformation is planned and designed where the course of the rough to perfect ashlars is devised  and calculated. This should not infer that the process is prescriptive; rather that it is descriptive as each individual is encouraged to approach it in his or her own way. The ritual stones and board in this ceremony serve to represent the shape the individual Mason will attain, as he applies its principals upon their own personal blue 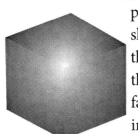 print. The allegory here in Masonic ritual is to shape and fit our selves, as individual stones, into the structure of the divine becoming a part of the whole. This function can be seen in the very fabric of Masonry itself, demonstrated so acutely in the notion of fraternal brotherhood.

Together these six jewels make up a helix of meaning representing purpose and process. But these symbolic elements are not solitary in their placement. An important symbol, represented simply in this tracing board, plays a prominent role in the application of all of these principals. So profound is its importance that it is said that every man made a mason is said to be represented in it and to make use of it through his whole life. That symbol is the point within the circle.

The importance of the point within the circle is such that it serves as a reminder for all masons of their material limitations of which they should measure with precision. Symbolically, it is said that Saint John the Baptist and Saint John the Evangelist flank the sides as reminders of the balance between zeal and knowledge of our fraternity. Their purpose is an external one, however, to the circle and its all-important point within. Specifically, the center point represents the individual mason surrounded by his moral boundary, as represented by the larger circle. This boundary is his own circumscribed limit to draw and not dictated by the fraternity or any other person. It is meant to represent his own moral boundary as supported by his faith, as he has come to know it. In the past, the Christian Bible crowned the Point within a circle, which served as the rule and moral guide to the drawn boundary, but today, as freemasonry has progressed, it recognizes the value of all faiths and that the absolution of the rule and guide can be can be several, but as is true of all faiths, it is grounded in basic tenants: a belief in the divine, the principals of the Golden Rule, and the tenants of Brotherly Love, Relief, and Truth.

These fundamental tenants of faith are the core of Freemasonry, and exist at the core of all faith traditions, which are represented in this tracing board by the inclusion of the thirteen faith tradition symbols[12] true Freemasonry being inclusive rather than exclusive. This position being stated in its doctrine of religious tolerance, as all faiths are valued and accepted in a lodge of Freemasonry.[13] This acceptance, in many ways is an ecumenical stance little observed in this modern age of fundamental demagoguery.

The importance of acceptance can be traced to its origin in Anderson's "old charges" which says: *"A Mason is oblig'd by his Tenure, to obey the moral law; and if he rightly understands the Art, he will never be a stupid Atheist nor an irreligious Libertine. But though in ancient Times Masons were charg'd in every Country to be of the Religion of that Country or Nation, whatever it was, yet 'tis now thought more expedient only to oblige them to that Religion in which all Men agree, leaving their particular Opinions to themselves; that is, to be good Men and true, or Men of Honor and Honesty, by whatever Denominations or Persuasions they may be distinguished; whereby Masonry becomes the Center of Union, and the Means of conciliating true Friendship among Persons that must have remain'd at a perpetual Distance"*. Some have come to believe that this position was likely an example of the practice of deism, common in that day, but like the practice of democracy in an era of the autocratic state, the idea of an ecumenical practice was very much ahead of its own time. Hermetic in nature, this idea is an acknowledgement and quest for the divine, which does not require specifically one divine nature, but rather the idea or acceptance of something beyond oneself.

Important to note here is an interpretation of the point within the circle, especially as it applies to its classical illustration. Visually, this is a simple pictograph, but it does not represent the progression of the initiate as other figures in this tracing board do.

Mentioned earlier in this description was the neophyte's entry into the sacred space upon and across the tessellated and checkered pavement. This movement is neither haphazard nor unregulated; rather it is to be perceived as a very specific progression from the west towards the east. Masonic tradition looks to Moses as being the first to erect a temple facing the east to commemorate the East wind that delivered the children of Israel from Egypt.[14] That tradition has been passed forward through the Jewish and Christian traditions, where the east is seen as the birthplace of knowledge, of life, and of death. Physically, it represents the rising of the sun, which has been seen as the origin of all things in many ancient cultures. Entry over this threshold brings the initiate towards the east, to the metaphorical rising sun, to the awakening of knowledge. Here is where we see the influence of Hermes, communicating to the initiated this sacred knowledge. There, on the board, at the center of everything is the blazing star of glory, which is the access point of his development, due east as the domain of the divine. It is towards that point the initiate seeks knowledge of the self.

Though the tools of the degree have been omitted, they too serve a specific role when conjoined with the artwork of the tracing board. The tools are the common gavel, which is used to shape and form the rough stones, the 24 inch gauge, which is made use of to measure and formulate the work to be performed, and the white lambskin apron, whose adornment symbolizes purity of spirit and intent, and whose color has symbolically been associated with the entry into the sacred space. These items would traditionally be presented to the candidate in the degree and not illustrated, as their roles are active, rather than passive and share elements of both the literal and figurative. Also not depicted in this illustration are the corner tassels, which serve as adornments to the tracing board. Four in total, the tassels represent the virtues of the candidate, which help to shape the circumscribed point within the circle. Those virtues are Temperance, (the resistance of affections and passions that can tempt to vice), Fortitude (strength of endurance both physical and mental challenges), Prudence (as the application of reason upon our lives) and Justice (giving us the standard of right and wrong as applied to civil society). These elements were omitted, as they are external to the candidate's internal progression as they are the merits by which to shape the living stone and the physical tools of the traveler. Each one is important and worthy of display as external adornments.

The transformational alchemy that this board represents is today symbolic in its gesture. There is no philosophers stone created, nor a transformation of led into gold performed. Instead what the alchemy of Freemasonry strives to make is the transformation of the untamed rough individual man towards a refined and controlled dressed stone contributing towards the betterment of his self and in course fitting into civil society. By these symbols and abstract conceptions, the first degree's purpose is to shape the initiates perception of the self and motivate them to begin a deeper understanding of their place and its relationship to the divine. This tradition of transformation, rendered by means of sacred geometry, alchemy, and representational allegory, has been handed down in time by both a conscious and unconscious means of communicating and instructing about the journey to the divine awakening and inner enlightenment for those who undergo its transformational rituals. An important aspect of this tracing board is the implied rule of three, which is further projected in the proceeding degrees culminating in the attainment of the "third degree" of a Master Mason, found in Craft Lodge Freemasonry. It is important to remember that the tracing board is only a visual representation of the actual ritual and degrees, and is in no way a substitute for the art and experience of undergoing it. The ancient traditions still involve the aspirant's decision to enter into the sacred space and without that physical decision, the ritual and symbolism become a jumble exotic shapes and broken illustrations. Like the Egyptian houses of Life, the beauty of tracing boards like this one is that they communicate forward the deeper meanings of our life through the degrees which enriches the experience of the initiate who can relate it to his own travels further facilitating the metaphoric movement into his own sacred space.

# XVIII
# FAITH IN
# FREEMASONRY

Mackey, in the *ENCYCLOPEDIA OF FREEMASONRY,* aptly (but narrowly) defines Faith as: *In the theological ladder, the explanation of which forms a part of the instruction of the First Degree of Masonry, faith is said to typify the lowest round. Faith, here, is synonymous with confidence or trust, and hence we find merely a repetition of the lesson which had been previously taught that the first essential qualification of a candidate for initiation is that he should trust in God. In the lecture of the same Degree, it is said that "Faith may be lost in sight; Hope ends in fruition; but Charity extends beyond the grave, through the boundless realms of eternity and this is said, because, as faith is "the evidence of things not seen," when we see we no longer believe by faith but through demonstration; and as hope lives only in the expectation of possession, it ceases to exist when the object once hoped for is at length enjoyed, but charity, exercised on earth in acts of mutual kindness and forbearance, is still found in the world to come, in the sublime form of mercy from God to his erring creatures.*

In the breadth of modern culture the definition of faith has come to be accepted as a belief in a transcendent reality, a heaven or Nirvana, often with the concept of a Supreme Being of other deific force as its focus. As the definition above suggests, it is a trust in a here after. A faith placed in the divine unseen.

Waite says of the symbol of faith in his *ENCYCLOPEDIA OF FREEMASONRY* that: *"... In the proper understanding, that Faith which according to St. Paul is the substance of things hoped for, [it] is the state that is desired by the wise, and seeing that Divine Faith can lead to Divine Attainment its profession with the whole heart and the whole will is the greatest act of wisdom which can be performed by man, because it leads into all truth and the great end of being...*

*...Faith is the loyalty of the human mind in adhesion to its own postulate concerning the truth of God, in virtue of which the mind cannot be stultified in following the quest of God..."*

Symbolically, the idea of faith has been represented in western society as the cross, or holy symbol that each of us hold as sacred. This emblem is symbolic of the faith of its bearer, and a testament to its owner's frame of spiritual reference. The idea of faith (as linked in Freemasonry with Hope and Charity) is found in I Corinthians 13, where St. Paul is teaches what creates unity or love amongst ones fellow believers. In Catholicism, the virtues have an older story that venerates the three virtues (faith, hope, and charity) as early Christian Saints in the second century who, along with their widowed mother Sophia (Sapientia), were martyred and then buried along the Apian Way.

The idea of faith though has a lineage that extends beyond a spiritual consciousness as we often place a degree of faith in many things. We see this as we place our own trust in things that we neither take the time to investigate or explore to derive a satisfactory answer. An example of this is how we come to accept aspects of science. Does gravity exist? What is air? We can experience its effects but can we actually see its operation? How many among us have taken the time to do the calculations to test what others have found? We trust in the knowledge of others to explain this phenomenon along with their operation and existence. This same analogy can be used as we examine what faith means and its extension to the unknown.

Readily we apply the term without fully grasping what this term "faith" means. To do this we need to look at the origin of the word and some of its early vestiges to see its meaning and how it may have come to be so readily associated with what we know it to be today.

Faith is now taken as belief in a transcendent reality, synonymous with belief and often interchangeable with the association of religion. We are, so often, seen as our faith (Christian, Jew, Hindu, Muslim etc…) especially as it connects us to the beliefs it espouses. Broadly used, this idea of faith is often interchangeable with trust, hope, and belief. This transcendental connection between the symbol and the faith it represents is evident in Christianity as faith is often a reflection of our salvation by a belief in the Christ, specifically as symbolized in the cross. The cross, a relative late adaptation of the faith, still finds resonance in its concept with a foundation reaching back to St. Augustine of Hippo [354-430 A.D.]. He proposed that all our beliefs rest ultimately on beliefs accepted by our faith, saying *"Crede, ut intelligas"* which translates to *"Believe in order that you may understand"* which is echoed in Mackey's definition of belief being "evidence of things not seen".

In the origin of the word faith however, we come to contrast in its connection to fideism whose definition is of a faith in philosophical and religious truths but to question its ability to answer ALL truths. Fideism has been used to delineate modern Protestant Christian faith as salvation by faith alone. Again, it is in this definition that contemporary Freemasonry seems to have taken a cue as to its base principal of what faith means. It is a faith in a hereafter that we put our trust in salvation and safety upon our passing. This idea of Fideism lends itself to the lessons of the degrees, as it is the spiritual revelation that we are taught in the 1º, but the scientific in the 2º as it extols the acquisition of knowledge in the liberal arts and sciences. This seems to be a distinct separation from a faith in deity and knowledge combined. Allegorically the study of the arts and sciences surly are a means to help define the divine and its work in this world giving us a hint at its handy work and operation.

To balance this notion of belief and knowledge, we need to take the idea of Fideism back a step to its origin in the word Fides, which as a Roman (Latin) word that means belief/trust (Fides is also suggested as one of the names of the martyred saints). But more than a blind trust the word was attributed to a Roman goddess where the word was

broadly used in the Roman world as *"Fides Publica Populi Romani"* (trust towards the Roman state) that would literally become the credo of Christianity towards the early Church. The mythology of Fides is that she (the goddess) was the young protector of Roman treaties that were held in her temple atop Capitoline Hill. This young goddess bore the emblem of the military in one hand, a cup in the other, and was crowned with an olive branch, which was, symbolically, the embodiment of the faith of the Roman world in the hands of the Empire. This still has a sense of trust, but in a broader sense by placing our trust in the agent of the Empire.

From here we can find an older origin that brought forth Fides essence, as we take the word into its Greek translation where Fides becomes the name Pistis or Pistis Sophia.

This translation is attributed to the Greek Gnostic text of the same name that relates the teachings of the transfigured Christ to his disciples. In this text Christ is said to of stayed 11 years with his disciples revealing his teachings. From the Berlin Codex of the Nag Hamadi Papyrus of the Gnostic books this Pistis Sophia reads:

*Again, his disciples said: Tell us clearly how they came down from the invisibilities, from the immortal to the world that dies?*

*The perfect Savior said: Son of Man consented with Sophia, his consort, and revealed a great androgynous light. Its male name is designated 'Savior, begetter of all things'. Its female name is designated 'All-begettress Sophia'. Some call her 'Pistis'.*

But, with the Gnostic/Christian story aside, we are given the term *Pistis Sophia* which is translated as *faith of Sophia*.

With this analysis, what stands out is this faith in Sophia, the mother of these martyred virtues. In the ancient Greek world, Sophia was said to be the embodiment of wisdom (communicated and known). The analysis of Sophia could go on at length, especially as it is a symbol that has traversed the ideas of several philosophies and belief systems where universally it has come to be synonymous with the idea of wisdom and knowledge, or the acquisition of knowledge. Even in the early martyrdom legend, the three virtues are said to be the children of Sophia, which makes for an interesting analogy to the ideas that surround faith, hope, and charity as coming from Wisdom.

*Pistis Sophia* becomes literally a faith from wisdom, which links us back to the second step of Freemasonry in the degrees. Faith, hope, and Charity being the vital lesson we learn in the 1° to be followed by a liberal approach to the acquisition of learning and knowledge. It is in this idea of *Pistis Sophia* that there is a strong relevance. Men do stand in faith, and many believe in their salvation for the simple fact that they believe. But so to is there a necessity of wisdom in which to guide our faith, that faith alone is just that, the empty aspect of believing and not knowing why, or what.

As we come to see the broader origin of the word and idea, we can start to construct the apparatus to allow ourselves to step beyond the constraints of faith for the sake of belief to explore the why of its depth. Faith, the strongest tool of the Freemason, deserves to be understood and not merely accepted as is given to him by our contemporary cultural understanding. Can we simply believe something because we are told we should? Mackey's definition bares weight as faith exists in "the evidence of things unseen, and that when we see, we no longer believe", but how do we come to see its invisible evidence? And only when we stop seeking that evidence will we cease to believe. By seeking Sophia, that wisdom and knowledge, those things to which we hold our faith inviolate can only then be understood. Through wisdom, we can coalesce our ideas of divine revelation into tangibles that we can then attribute as a part of our faith. Only then will we truly find the meanings and strength behind the sacred symbols that we make inviolate to our beliefs. And by continually seeking we will not "lose faith in sight" of what we pursue to be absolutes.

Jacob Matham nach Hendrick Goltzius 1558 - 1616
Die sieben Tugenden [The Seven virtues]:
*Fides (Die Treue - Faithfulness)*
Engraving

# XIX
# HOPE IN
# FREEMASONRY

Mackey in the *ENCYCLOPEDIA OF FREEMASONRY* aptly defines Hope in Freemasonry: *HOPE - The second round in the theological and Masonic ladder, and symbolic of a hope in immortality. It is appropriately placed there, for, having attained the first, or faith in God, we are led by a belief in His wisdom and goodness to the hope of immortality. This is but a reasonable expectation; without it, virtue would lose its necessary stimulus and vice its salutary fear; life would be devoid of joy, and the grave but a scene of desolation. The ancients represented Hope by a nymph or maiden holding in her hand a bouquet of opening flowers, indicative of the coming fruit; but in modern and Masonic iconology, the science of Craft illustrations and likenesses, it is represented by a virgin leaning on an anchor, the anchor itself being a symbol of hope.*

The idea of hope is much older and specific though. Defined in a modern sense, hope is a belief in a positive outcome relating to events and circumstances in life. It is the desire that something will turn out for the best. From a spiritual context it is an awareness of a "spiritual truth" as from a virtue as from an older stand point, hope comes from the Catholic idea of the three virtues "faith, hope, and charity" and are given to us as gifts from God. It is more of a positive way of thinking once all action has been taken for the outcome desired, including prayer.

But hope has an even older origin, dating back into antiquity of Greek mythology and the story of Pandora.

In mythology, Pandora was the first woman created by the gods who gave to her unique gifts (attributes). After man having received the gift of fire from Prometheus, an angry Zeus decides to punish him by giving him the gift of woman to compensate for the boon they had been given. He orders Hephaestus to form from earth the first woman, a work of "beautiful evil", whose descendants would forever torment man. After Hephaestus does so, Athena dressed her in a silvery gown, an embroidered veil, garlands and an ornate crown of gold.

In the Greek poem *"Works and Days"*, the story of Pandora continues and tells of her marriage to Epimetheus, the brother of Prometheus, where Pandora was given many seductive gifts from Aphrodite, Hermes, Charites, and Horae. Zeus, being mischievous, gave Pandora a large jar [box] and instructs her to keep it closed. But in her creation, she was given the gift of curiosity and succumbed to opening it despite the warning.

Once opened, all of the evil spirits it contained spewed out into the world, all of the ills, burdens, strife, fear, horror, pestilence, disease, and labor that had, up to that point been unknown to mankind. In her shock, she closed the box trapping and the last spirit within, hope. At some point later, she returns to the box and opens it at last freeing hope to the world.

Hope, as it existed in this story was the last of the evils to be let out and is associated with the other evils, which means it could be construed to be when taken in a false sense when it emerges it is a small and weak spirit seemingly incapable of compare to the previous evils already unleashed. That weakness however is quickly turned to the greatest of strengths as it brought with it a means for mankind to deal with and see though the evils set loose upon it. This could be perceived as it gave mankind the resolve to put their faith in a divine force to triumph, even if holding off giving up over the ills and powers against them.

Masonicly, Pike says of Hope in *MORALS IN DOGMA* as it relates to the dimensions of the Lodge, *"our Brethren of the York Rite say,* *"are unlimited, and its covering no less than the canopy of Heaven."* *"To this object,"* they say, *"the mason's mind is continually directed, and thither he hopes at last to arrive by the aid of the theological ladder which Jacob in his vision saw ascending from earth to Heaven; the three principal rounds of which are denominated Faith, Hope, and Charity; and which admonish us to have Faith in God, Hope in Immortality, and Charity to all mankind."*

In more modern times, the idea of hope has been explored to find its lengths and meaning. Nietzsche suggests that hope is from Zeus so that man will forever allow himself to be tormented buy having it. Emily Dickenson referred to it as a thing with feathers that rests upon the soul. In more recent times it has been suggested that the Utopian ideal is an expression of hope as an unachievable end, but a thing to strive towards. More recently in modern exploration the idea of hope has challenged that the idea of hope as a thing of little effect on ones life but rather as a necessary [evil] component of survival, as without hope (hopelessness) we will undo our well being

which interestingly ties back into the story of Pandora as her release of hope gives us some measure to combat the evils we face in the world.

From the Masonic perspective, we have tied the notion of hope to the interaction of the divine to those things that we cannot effect, which seems to link back to the stance of the church in our hope for immortality. But, when taking it in light of the emptied Pandora's Box we can connect it on a deeper level to a point disconnected from religiosity and divine inspiration and humanize it as a belief unto itself. Having done all that out actions can allow we can stand fast to the belief in hope that somehow we, in our spirit and work will prevail. In this coupling of spirit and action we can connect the compass to the square to the points where the celestial meets the firmament.

In my own study of Masonic symbolism, I have found resonance with Mackey's mention of the anchor and the ark as they seem to relate in that the ark is where we abode for safety in the storm and derive resolution by the anchor for our decisions. With the addition of faith and charity we can formulate our triumphs over the evils set before us by Pandora's Box that worry the world.

Jacob Matham nach Hendrick Goltzius 1558 - 1616
Faith, Hope, and Charity
Engraving

# XX
# CHARITY IN FREEMASONRY

Charity, and its meaning in Freemasonry is well encapsulated by Mackey as defined in his Encyclopedia with this opening quote from the Christian Volume of the Sacred law:

> *"Though I speak with the tongues of men and of angels, and have not charity, I am become as sounding brass, or a tinkling cymbal.*
>
> *And though I have the gift of prophecy, and understand all mysteries and all knowledge; and though I have all faith, so that I could remove mountains, and have not charity, I am nothing"*
> **1 Corinthians 8:1-2.**

Mackey's entry into his encyclopedia goes on to define Masonic Charity, saying:

> *Such was the language of an eminent apostle of the Christian church, and such is the sentiment that constitutes the cementing bond of Freemasonry. The apostle, in comparing it with faith and hope, calls it the greatest of the three, and hence in Freemasonry it is made the topmost round of its mystic ladder.*

*We must not fall into the too common error that charity is only that sentiment of commiseration which leads us to assist the poor with pecuniary donations.*

*Its Masonic, as well as its Christian application, is nobler and more extensive.*

*The word used by the apostle is, in the original, love, a word denoting that kindly state of mind which renders a person full of good-will and affectionate regards toward others.*

*John Wesley[1] expressed his regret that the Greek had not been correctly translated as love instead of charity, so that the apostolic triad of virtues would have been, not "faith, hope, and charity," but "faith, hope, and love."*

*Then would we have understood the comparison made by Saint Paul, when he said, "Though I bestow all my goods to feed the poor, and though I give my body to be burned, and have not love, it profited me nothing."[2]*

*Guided by this sentiment, the true Freemason will "suffer long and be kind."*

*He will be slow to anger and easy to forgive.*

*He will stay his falling Brother by gentle admonition, and warn him with kindness of approaching danger; he will not open his ear to the slanderers, and will lose his lips against all reproach.*

*His faults and his follies will be locked in his breast, and the prayer for mercy will ascend to Jehovah for his Brother's sins.*

*Nor will these sentiments of benevolence be confined to those who are bound to him by ties of kindred or worldly friendship alone; but, extending them throughout. the globe, he will love and cherish all who sit beneath the broad canopy of our universal Lodge.*

*For it is the boast of our Institution, that a Freemason, destitute and worthy, may find in every clime a Brother, and in every land a home.*

Mackey goes on to a quote from the time of the Civil War which gives us a glimpse from the past of what just such a Charity (love) looks like saying:

*Colonel Edward M L. Ehlers, a soldier of the Civil War in which he was severely wounded, was subsequently and at his death the Grand Secretary of New York.*

*To his courtesy and promptness the reviser of this work is much indebted for many favors and there is a distinct satisfaction in submitting here one of the eloquent addresses to initiates that so often heartened his hearers (see Definitions of Freemasonry).*

*My Brother: With this right hand I welcome you to the fellowship of our Lodge and to the ranks of our ancient and honorable Fraternity whose cornerstone is Charity.*

*Charity is the brightest jewel in the Masonic crown.*

*Charity is the Corinthian pillar whose entablature adds strength, beauty and grace to the Masonic fabric.*

*Charity is the radiant spark emanating from God, the inexhaustible source of love.*

*If we attempt to eulogize its charms, the cooler powers of the mind melt into ecstasy, the heart is at empire, and every discordant passion bows before its lenient sovereignty.*

*Not the Charity circumscribed by the narrow limits of feeding the hungry, clothing the naked, binding up the wounds of the afflicted, but that broader nobler Charity that regards all men as Brothers.*

*The Charity that is swift of foot, ready of hand, in the cause of a common humanity.*

*The Charity that writes a Brother's vices in water and his virtues in enduring brass.*

*The Charity of which He who spake as never man spake was the illustrious exemplar.*

*Let this, the Mason's Charity, burn upon the altar of your heart a living fire.*

*This Charity whose superstructure is friendship, morality, brotherly love; whose capstone is holiness to the Lord. Liturgies and creeds, articles of faith and rules of discipline, stain the rubric pages of history, and speculative points of doctrine have occasioned more misery in the world than all the crimes for which nations have been punished and recalled to their duty.*

*We arrange no man's political opinions, nor do we interfere with his religious creed.*

*To himself and his country we leave the one, and to his conscience and his God we commit the other. To the altar of Masonry, all men bring their votive offerings. Around it all men, whether they have received their teachings from Confucius, Moses, Zoroaster, Mahomet, or the Founder of the Christian religion; if they believe in the universality of the Fatherhood of God and of the universality of the brotherhood of man, here meet on a common level.*

*The rich man, the poor man, the sovereign, the subject, are lost in the common Brother. The Christian returns to his Temple, the Jew to his Synagogue, the Mohammedan to his Mosque, each better prepared to perform the duties of life by the association of this universal brotherhood. It is to this Institution, born of heaven in the gray of the world's morning, before poets sang or historians wrote that I am privileged to accord you a Craftsman's greeting.*

*And I charge you, by the noblest instincts of your manhood, by all that you are and revere, by the ties that bind you to earth, by your hope of heaven, so to live and so to act that your Masonic life may be an open book known and read of all men.*

*Finally, my Brother, I do assure you that whatever good you do is but duty done.*

*If a sorrow you have lightened or a tear wipe away, if of poverty's load you have taken a share from some weary burdened soul, if you have lifted a cup of cold water to the lips of a famishing mortal, then to far have you illustrated the divine teachings of Masonry, then in so far have you done as the Master commanded.*

*May He, without whose knowledge not even a sparrow falls, bless your fellowship in our Lodge and to His great name shall be all the praise.*

This long definition, with its extensive quotations, sums nicely the broader meaning of what we today manifest in our institutional charity. In short, we can see that its meaning goes beyond the institutional giving that has become the principal result of our expression of love where today it is the expression that has become the symbol of love. This meaning is brought forth from the Christian tradition that we find in 1st Corinthians as its translation implies a deeper love and that without we are nothing.

But, to facilitate this understanding, let us first dig deeper into the origin of the word charity, and from that point derive a means of its application, or at least formulate a means to know how to understand it.

From the Christian tradition, we find the idea of charity comes from the Greek word agape, which was a term seldom used in more ancient manuscripts. Its Greek meaning was of a deep affection, in the time of Plato[3], using it to infer a love of a spouse or family, or an affection towards a particular activity. It is in the Christian application where it is broadened into a self sacrificing love of God for humanity, where the practice of it became a self reciprocating act towards the divine. Simply, we have a love and affection for God, thereby we love all of God's children (humanity).

In the few ancient usages we can trace the word into the Odyssey by Homer, but in variations as "agapeton" and "agapazomenoi", whose meanings are viewed as "beloved" and "to treat with affection" respectively. Also, the word appears in the Septuagint which is the oldest of several translations of the Greek Hebrew bible, translated into Latin between the 3rd and 1st centuries B.C.E. in Alexandria. In this text we find the usage of "agapao" which is again to reflect as a love for a beloved husband/wife/child, a brotherly love, and God's love for humanity. It is from this text that it is believed to have moved into the usage of Christian writers in the New Testament.

In this more recent Christian application, agape was made to reflect more of a love, as defining God as love, a brotherly love, a love of family, and the love of God for humanity.[4]

This later usage too is perceived to mean a form of love that is both unconditional as it is voluntary, as the Christ saying in the Sermon on the mount in the Gospel of Matthew:

*"You have heard that it was said, 'Love your neighbor and hate your enemy.' But I tell you: Love your enemies and pray for those who persecute you, that you may be sons of your Father in heaven. He causes his sun to rise on the evil and the good, and sends rain on the righteous and the unrighteous. If you love those who love you, what reward will you get? Are not even the tax collectors doing that? And if you greet only your brothers, what are you doing more than others? Do not even pagans do that? Be perfect, therefore, as your heavenly Father is perfect."*
***Matthew 5:43-48 N.I.V.***

The love that Matthew is espousing is this agape form of love, loving because it is how God loves.

Roman Charity is the tale of a daughter, Pero, who secretly breastfeeds her father, Cimon, after he is sentenced to death by starvation. Found out by a jailer, her act of selflessness impresses officials and wins her father's release.

It is in this broader sense that we can read from Mackey how it is explored in Masonry, as a broader love of all, both unconditionally and of our own will. It is in this full extent that we have come to translate agape into what we define today as charity. In the early organization of the church, theologians wove the idea of charity in with the other muses of faith, hope, and their mother

Sophia (the latter as the representation of wisdom). In this story, we find the young martyred muse Charitas of whom the virtue is to be extolled. It is in her name that we find the origin of the word charity today.

From this Latin appellation, caritas, we have associated to it a preciousness, dearness (as a family), and the valuation of as a high price, but in the church translation into Latin, it became the definition of the Greek word agape, as meaning an "unlimited loving kindness, to all others, such as the love of God. Perhaps this could be extended to see those worthy of kindness to be the meek, and consequently the inheritors of the earth.[5]

How the word evolved, however, is a mystery of time. What we find is that the word charity entered the English language through the Old French word "charite" which was derived from the Latin "Caritas", our martyred saint.

As the word through scriptures has matured, its meaning has evolved and taken on an existence of its own, especially as it has come to represent the manifestation of love rather than the very act of loving. In the middle ages, the act of this love became the giving of alms, whereby the act of loving was professed in the giving of money or time to the unfortunate, infirm, or destitute. It seems that the meaning of this word from agape was changed to become the act of charitable giving as a representation of this love. Through this alms giving, the receivers were seen as those most in need to receive them. But it is in this giving that, I believe, a disconnect occurs, as it is not seen as a filial[6] giving (as to family) but rather a disconnected care to strangers who are otherwise without affection. Essentially becoming a loving of those unloved.

It is in this much later practice of alms giving to those unrelated that we find much of the fraternal meaning we see today.

It is a stretch to find the idea of an agape style love (affection) to mankind rather than an alms giving form of institutional charity. As the word evolves, perhaps so to does the ideation of it as the circular extension of this agape style appellation of genuine affection for all of the children of God which is significantly changed. Is there still room to love beyond the fold of immediate family, or are we merely mistaking the broader spectrum of what that love could be?

To get a salient image of these three muses from wisdom one thought coalesces that seems imperative to take them together where the allegories and symbols of Freemasonry have them by themselves. Faith, Hope, and Charity, the children of wise widowed mother Sophia, create an interesting sphere of ideology and oneness as a manifestation of Divine providence. Through belief we can envision, with hope we can understand, and by charity(agape) we can love, all of which are borne out of wisdom, out of Sophia the widowed mother, and in their totality put us in communion with out own divine spirit.

Drawing from these other traditions, perhaps we can contrast them with the Grand Master Hiram Abiff as the physical manifestation of the muses, and as the operative side of their ideal, as he too is the allegorical child of the widow martyred for his belief. By connecting these two disparate parts we form a bridge from the spiritual to the material, especially when we see them with Jacob's ladder, as this becomes the path of transcendence. On another level, Hiram is the earthly manifestation of the spirit of Sophia (wisdom) betrayed by his brothers in pursuit of the knowledge (gnosis) that he holds. This does present a juxtaposition of his betrayal at the demand of knowledge rather than through its pursuit, which allegorically leads us to the ladder. By applying love, we will then learn the secret, rather which demand its gifts.

How ever we look at the muses, and in particular charity, in this new light of agapeton, meaning unlimited loving kindness, the words of Colonel Ehleers and from 1 Corinthians stand in an even stronger resonance when taken as Mackey indicated, connecting John Wesley's translation saying:

*When I was a child, I spake as a child, I understood as a child, I thought as a child: but when I became a man, I put away childish things.*

*For now we see through a glass, darkly; but then face to face: now I know in part; but then shall I know even as also I am known.*

*And now abideth faith, hope, charity, these three; but the greatest of these is charity (love).*
*I Corinthians 5:11-13*

For truth, the greatest strength of mankind and Freemasonry is the true meaning of agape-charity which is love. How it is manifested, or how we express that meaning from our lessons of faith or from the degrees of Freemasonry, is at our hand and their truest meaning is of love.

Jacob Matham nach Hendrick Goltzius 1558 - 1616
Die sieben Tugenden [The Seven virtues]:
*Charitas (Die Liebe - Love)*
Engraving

# FOOTNOTES

Chapter III - The Beehive.

1. Hayward, H.L. 1948. *The Newly Made Mason*. Richmond: Macoy Publishing. p.#213

2. Duncan, Malcom C. Third Edition (undated). *Duncan's Masonic Ritual and Monitor*. New York: Crown Publishers. p.#128


Chapter IV - Anno Lucis.

1. Grand Lodge of British Colombia, "http://freemasonry.bcy.ca/aqc/anno_lucis/anno_lucis.html" British Colombia, Canada.   An excellent reference to subject.

2. Ibid.


Chapter VIII - Religion of not being a religion.

1. Pike, Albert. 1871. *Morals and Dogma of the Ancient and Accepted Scottish Rite of Freemasonry*. richmond: L.H. Jenkins. p.#161-2

2. Shaw, James D.  1988. *The Deadly Deception: Freemasonry Exposed by One of Its Top Leaders*. Layafette: Huntington House.

3. Taxil, Léo. 1892. *La France chrétienne anti-maçonnique*.

## Chapter IX. - Freemasonry in Modern Art

1. See Shag's website http://www.shag.com for his most recent work. Also see *Shag Ltd. Fine Art Limited Editions*, published in 2005 by Douglas Nelson, published by Copro Gallery, Santa Monica.

2. Stevens, Ray. 1980. *Shriner's Convention* song and video. http://www.youtube.com/watch?v=YRC2fdDVMiI (pulled 11/2009)

3. Mastodon. 2006. *Blood and Thunder* – song and video, from the album Leviathan. http://www.youtube.com/watch?v=labytsb3gfI (pulled 11/2009)

## Chapter XI. - Hermetic Tradition and America

1. Copenhaver, Brian P. 2000. Hermetica. Cambridge: University Press. p.# xiv "megistou kai megistou theou megalou Hermou"

2. The earliest source of the Emerald Tablet is the Kitab sirr al-Asrar from 940 A.D., translated into latin as Secretum Secretorum in 1140A.D.

3. Churton, Tobias. 2005. *The Golden Builders*. New York: Weiser Books.

4. Matthew 5:14 N.I.V. - *"You are the light of the world. A city on a hill cannot be hidden."*

## Chapter XII. - Freemasonry and the Kybalion

1. Otherwise known as B.O.T.A. which is *"Builders of the Adytum is a modern Mystery School."* "Adytum is the Greek word for Inner Shrine or Holy of Holies. Like Jesus, who many believe was trained in Qabalah, members of the Order aspire to build the Inner Temple, to construct the Holy of Holies within. People of all faiths are welcome to study the teachings of this Order. B.O.T.A. recognizes Qabalah as the root of Judaism and Christianity. Its ultimate purpose is to hasten the true Brotherhood of mankind and to make manifest the truth that love is the only real power in the universe." http://www.bota.org

2. Hall, Manly P. 1928/2003 *The Secret Teachings of All Ages*. New York: Tarcher/Penguin. *"The Pythagorean Theory of Music and Color"* p. # 81

## Chapter XIII. - So What?

1. *The Masonic Service Association of North America* http://www.msana.com/

2. Knights of the North. 2006. *Laudable Pursuit*. Lulu.com.

3. For example the O.T.O., The Golden Dawn, Builders of the Adytum, AMORC Rosicrucianism.

## Chapter XIV. - King Solomon's Temple

1. Hodapp, Christopher. 2005. *Freemasons for Dummies*. New Jersey: Wiley Publishing, Inc.

2. Yates, Frances. 1979/2003. *The Occult Philosophy in the Elizabethan Age*. London/New York: Routledge.

3. MacNaulty, W. Kirk. 1991. *A Journey Through Ritual and Symbol*. London, Thames and Hudson.

4. Morgan, Morris Hickey. 1960. *Vitruvius, 10 Books on Architecture*. New York: Dover.

5.Duncan, Malcom C. Third Edition (undated). *Duncan's Masonic Ritual and Monitor*. New York: Crown Publishers. p.#74

## Chapter XV. - St. John the Baptist

1. New Advent Catholic Encyclopedia. *"Saint John the Baptist,"* http://www.newadvent.org/cathen/08486b.htm (accessed 11/2009)

## Chapter XVI. - St. John the Evangelist

1. New Advent Catholic Encyclopedia. *"Saint John the Evangelist,"* http://www.newadvent.org/cathen/08492a. htm (accessed 11/2009) - The feast of St. John before the Latin Gate, supposed to commemorate the dedication of the church near the Porta Latina, is first mentioned in the Sacramentary of Adrian I (772-95)

## Chapter XVII. - 1° Masonic Tracing Board

1. Anderson, James. 1738. *Anderson's Constitution*. Whitefish: Kessinger Publishing. p# 109

2. Churton, Tobias. 2005. *The Golden Builders*. New York: Weiser Books. p.# 36-37

3. Ibid.

4. Copenhaver, Brian P. 2000. *Hermetica*. Cambridge: University Press. p# 1

4. Occult, Obscured: from the Latin word occultus (hidden, obscured, clandestine, secret), as in a "knowledge of the unseen". Relating to a deeper spiritual understanding.

5. I Kings 6 - K.J.V. *And it came to pass in the four hundred and eightieth year after the children of Israel were come out of the land of Egypt, in the fourth year of Solomon's reign over Israel, in the month Zif, which is the second month, that he began to build the house of the LORD.*

6. First set destroyed by Moses Exodus 34 - NIV: *The LORD said to Moses, "Chisel out two stone tablets like the first ones, and I will write on them the words that were on the first tablets, which you broke.*

7. Yates, Frances. 1972/2003. *Rosicrucian Enlightenment*. London/New York: Routledge. p.# 267

8. MacNaulty, W. Kirk. 1991. *A Journey Through Ritual and Symbol*. London, Thames and Hudson. p. #21

9. Morgan, Morris Hicky. 1960. *Vitruvius - 10 Books on Archatecture*. New York:Bover Publications. p.# 13

10. Duncan, Malcom C. Third Edition (undated). *Duncan's Masonic Ritual and Monitor*. New York: Crown Publishers. p. #36

11. Bahai, Buddhism, Zoroastrianism, Shinto, I Ching, Jainism, Taoism, Islam, Judaism, Freemasonry, Christianity, Hinduism, Sikhism, Wiccan

12. Anderson, James. 1738. *Anderson's Constitution.* Whitefish: Kessinger Publishing.

*Concerning GOD and RELIGION: A Mason is oblig'd by his Tenure, to obey the moral law; and if he rightly understands the Art, he will never be a stupid Atheist nor an irreligious Libertine. But though in ancient Times Masons were charg'd in every Country to be of the Religion of that Country or Nation, whatever it was, yet 'tis now thought more expedient only to oblige them to that Religion in which all Men agree, leaving their particular Opinions to themselves; that is, to be good Men and true, or Men of Honour and Honesty, by whatever Denominations or Persuasions they may be distinguish'd; whereby Masonry becomes the Center of Union, and the Means of conciliating true Friendship among Persons that must have remain'd at a perpetual Distance.*

13. Matthew 24:27 - *For as the lightning comes from the east and shines as far as the west, so will be the coming of the Son of man.*

Numbers 3:38- *Moses and Aaron and his sons were to camp to the east of the tabernacle, toward the sunrise, in front of the Tent of Meeting. They were responsible for the care of the sanctuary on behalf of the Israelites. Anyone else who approached the sanctuary was to be put to death.*

Ezekiel 43:1-6- *Then the man brought me to the gate facing east, and I saw the glory of the God of Israel coming from the east. His voice was like the roar of rushing waters, and the land was radiant with his glory. The vision I saw was like the vision I had seen when he came to destroy the city and like the visions I had seen by the Kebar River, and I fell facedown. The glory of the LORD entered the temple through the gate facing east. Then the Spirit lifted me up and brought me into the inner court, and the glory of the LORD filled the temple.*

## Chapter XX. - Charity in Freemasonry

1. Global Ministries , *"The Sermons of John Wesley"* On Charity, By John Wesley, Sermon 91, "http://new.gbgm-umc.org/umhistory/wesley/sermons/91/" (accessed 11/2009)

2. I. Corinthians 13:1 - NIV: *If I speak in the tongues of men and of angels, but have not love, I am only a resounding gong or a clanging cymbal.*

3. See Plato's Symposium as man may arrive at a higher degree of good, both an intuitive and mystical state of consciousness.

4. John 4:16 - K.J.V. - *And we have known and believed the love that God hath to us. God is love; and he that dwelleth in love dwelleth in God, and God in him.*

5. Matthew 5:5 K.J.V. - *Blessed are the meek: for they shall inherit the earth.*

6. Middle English, from Late Latin filialis, from Latin filius son

# HAVE YOU VISITED THE NEW FREEMASON INFORMATION WEB SITE?

## http://www.freemasoninformation.com

Freemason Information is a Masonic web magazine for both Freemasons and those interested in the fraternity of Freemasonry.

FmI's web sites principal aim is to provide a means to discuss, explore, and provide commentary about the modern craft, its role in society, and areas of interest to the fraternities diverse membership. Its also seeks to bring interesting news from within the fraternity and without to create a working space for Masonic thought leaders, active lodges, and interested members to discover what is taking place in the fraternity beyond the 4 walls of their lodge room.

Freemason Information also exists to broaden the understanding of non Masons who have an interest in the fraternity. While each Grand Lodge should speak for Freemasonry in its respective state, FmI offers a broad overview to the organization and its many components that stretch around the globe.

While at the site you can download the FREE ebook "What is Freemasonry?". Also you can listen to the Masonic Central pod cast which is a weekly web audio program dedicated to all things Masonic.

We invite you to come for a visit, spend some time, and delve into the many aspects of the ancient and honorable fraternity.

# Now you can own the beautifully illustrated Tracing Board featured in this book.

## http://masonictraveler.imagekind.com

In the galleries you can find all three Masonic Tracing Boards and esoteric works made through the electronic digital medium.

This artwork is dedicated to the further discovery of the Light within in Freemasonry.

Its goal and purpose is to pursue a personal understanding of the divine in the context of the relativism of man and his nihilistic individuality.

Truly, this artwork is an expression of Freemasonry in digital art. Each tracing boards is an original work created by Greg Stewart who's goal was to create a contemporary translation of the allegorical degrees of Blue Lodge Freemasonry.

Stop by, have a look at the art, and discover some of the symbolic nuance of the degrees that you may not have seen before.

LaVergne, TN USA
07 September 2010
196122LV00007B/124/P

9 780615 359182